Runaway

Life on the Streets:
The Lessons Learned

by

Roger Dean Kiser

authorHOUSE®

AuthorHouse™
1663 Liberty Drive, Suite 200
Bloomington, IN 47403
www.authorhouse.com
Phone: 1-800-839-8640

First published by AuthorHouse 8/30/2007

ISBN: 978-1-4343-3566-1 (sc)

Printed in the United States of America
Bloomington, Indiana

This book is printed on acid-free paper.

Appreciation

I want to thank the people I met on the streets, though there were few who were kind enough to help me—individuals who owned only the clothes on their back, yet shared and helped a very confused young boy, expecting nothing in return for the kindness shown to him.

Your kindnesses, remembered by me, live on into the future. Through the years, I have helped many who chose your lifestyle. Though I am now the one bringing food and clothing, it was you who taught me to share and care for others less fortunate than myself.

What did I get out of it all?

I turned out to be a man with a kind heart, a man who learned from a few that he was not the "stupid bastard" that the orphanage had convinced him he was. That was a wonderful day in my life.

Dedication

I dedicate this book to the memory of James Byrd, Jr. of Jasper, Texas. A fine young man who will remain in my memory until my dying day.

I would like to dedicate this book to the children of tomorrow—to the kids who will one day run away because they did not get to go to the mall with their friends, and to the hundreds of kids who run away each year because Mom and Dad wanted them to do their homework or empty the garbage, to the ones who will destroy their lives by thinking that freedom and happiness lie just beyond the next street, the next alley or the next city.

I hope by reading my stories, they will realize that running away today is only going to make them unhappy for many, many tomorrows.

Contents

Introduction

While I suppose that the world is a much more dangerous place today than when I lived on the streets many years ago, there were times I found myself in great danger. Several times, I was lucky to have escaped with my life, and there were a few kids that were not so lucky. However, I must admit, I met many wonderful people during my adventures up and down the alleyways of Jacksonville, Florida.

There were times when those who had very little shared equally with me. That taught me much about the kindness of others. Then there were those who, like wild animals, would prey upon others and leave them for dead. The perverts came in all shapes and sizes. Some were bums, while some were police officers; here and there a lawyer, a schoolteacher and even a juvenile judge. I learned much about the world from these wicked, self-serving people. I cannot count the times I saw police officers do horrible and unthinkable things to other human beings— all because these individuals did not measure up to the standards set forth by certain upstanding members of the community.

Considering all that happened to me, I did not turn out to be a bad person. I just turned out to be a man who believes in very little, finds it very difficult to love, trust, or take the word of his fellow man.

Were all those lonely days and nights of living on the streets worth the negative feelings I live with today as an adult? Were those who sexually abused me the same ones who now cause the pain I feel as a man? Should I have continued to face the orphanage abuses for a few more years, in order to be happy when my adult life finally arrived?

I do not know the answers to those questions.

Raised in the Children's Home Society Orphanage in Jacksonville, Florida, I have no memory—not even one day—of what it is like to have a mother or a father. I was just there, living in that prison, day after day, year after year. I sat staring at walls and rocking back and forth. From age five to fourteen, I learned absolutely nothing. Had I stayed in that prison, what was there for me in the outside world once I walked out the gates? Upon leaving, all I would have known how to build was a "prison life" for the family that I would one day acquire. How does one build a happy, stable family home, if he does not have the slightest idea how one is constructed, or what such a home even feels like? Is there a purpose in having a home, other than to provide shelter?

A boy cannot prepare himself to travel to the moon once he becomes a man if no one ever teaches him such a thing exists. At eighteen, he will walk out of the orphanage having no idea what he is supposed to be looking for. Should he look up and notice the moon, he will have no idea what it represents, what purpose it serves or what value it has to his life.

Was living on the streets better than that type of life? Did I make the right choices? Did I destroy my own life by the choices I made during childhood? Was it I, and no one else, who made me an unhappy adult? Again, I do not know the answers to those questions. What I do know is that if I had not taken to the streets, I would have had no life at all. I would have sat there in that orphanage, becoming nothing more than a vegetable.

The stories in this book tell of the lessons I learned while living on the streets. The good, the bad and the ugly experiences allowed me to learn about respect, consideration, honesty and survival. The hobo camps and back alleys of the city taught me much. I learned how to feed, clothe and care for myself. I learned to build a fire for warmth on a cold day. I learned how to protect myself, not only from the bad in our society, but also from those who appear to be good and just.

Without this knowledge, I would have had no experiences to build a life for myself. I would not be able to survive in today's world, because then I would only have known how to survive in an incarcerated environment—places like jails and prisons, places where one does not have to think for himself, where one simply sits around all day, fed, clothed and housed. I was nothing more than a product in a store window, an item that could never be purchased. The orphanage received state funds every month to keep me displayed on the shelf. Those funds for my care became the sole purpose that they allowed me to live.

Maybe things would have been different if I had had a family, or if the orphanage had taken the time to teach me something useful and beneficial. Did I make the right choice? Under the circumstances, I think I did.

I had only two choices. I did not have the options that most other children have—things like parents, brothers, sisters, a refrigerator, my own room, a TV, a sandwich when I was hungry. I did not have the right to get a drink of water or use the bathroom without asking permission.

Not once did I ever own a shirt, a pair of pants, or even one pair of socks that belonged to me and me alone. As a child, I never owned one toy of my own. I had absolutely nothing to live for, and I felt I had nothing to lose, except my life. And it was a life that was useless and meaningless to everyone, including me. My choices were limited. I could risk my life living on the streets, or I could stay in the orphanage and become a wilted vegetable.

I would never endorse telling a child to head out into the streets to live. To me, my situation became one of survival. If the orphanage had not beaten me to death, they would have mentally destroyed me. I did not run away because I did not get to go to the mall. I did not run away because I had to eat pancakes for supper, rather than the tacos I desired. I ran away because there were no other options open to me. Even when being sexually molested, there was absolutely no one that I could turn to for help. No one would believe that adults would do such horrible things to children—not my teachers, not the church minister, and not even the police. The Children's Home Society Orphanage in Florida, together with the Juvenile Court, was the only word that mattered. They were "The Supreme Being."

I felt cornered on top of a 200-foot-high bridge, with five pit bulls chewing at my legs. I had to make a dangerous choice. Do I stand here and die, or do I jump and die? I chose to jump. I guess taking to the streets was a price that this little boy had to pay.

Wishes

Once upon a time, a lifetime ago, when I was a little boy who lived in an orphanage in Jacksonville, Florida, I had always wished that I could fly like a bird. It was very difficult for me to understand why I could not fly, 'cause then I could go find my very own mother and father. There were birds at the zoo that were much bigger than I, and they could fly.

"Why can't I?" I thought. "Is there something wrong with me?"

One day I met a little boy who was crippled. He had always wished that he could walk and run like all the other little boys and girls.

"Why can't I be like them?" he thought.

One day when I ran away from the orphanage, I came upon a park. That is when I saw that little boy who could not walk, playing in the sandbox. I went over to the boy and asked him if he had ever wanted to fly like a bird.

"No," said the little boy, who could not walk or run. "But I have wondered what it would be like to walk, run and play like other little boys and girls," he told me.

"That is very sad. Do you think we could be friends?" I asked the little boy, who was playing in the sandbox.

"Sure. I really need a friend," said the little boy.

We played together for hours. We made sandcastles, and we made funny sounds with our mouths, sounds that made us laugh really hard. Then the little boy's father came with a wheelchair to pick up his son. I stood up, brushed myself off and ran over to the boy's father. I asked him to bend down so that I could whisper something into his ear.

"That would be okay, I guess," said the man.

I ran over to my new friend and said, "You are my only friend, and I wish that there was something that I could do to make you walk and run like other little boys and girls. I can't, but there is one thing I can do for you."

I turned around and told my new friend to slide up onto my back. Then I began to run across the grass as fast as I could. Faster and faster I ran, carrying the crippled little boy on my back. Harder and harder, I pushed across the park. Faster and faster, I made my legs travel until they hurt. I ran in a never-ending circle around the boy's father and the old wheelchair.

Soon the wind silently whistled across our little faces, gliding past us as though we were both large eagles, soaring above the highest mountains.

The boy's father began to cry as he watched his beautiful crippled son, riding on my back, flapping his arms up and down in the wind, while all the time yelling and screaming at the top of his voice, "I am flying, daddy. I am flying!"

A Nickel's Worth

What a scared seven-year-old boy I was, when after two days, the orphanage finally let me out of that dark closet. I took my bath, brushed my teeth with soap, and dressed myself for school in the clothes that the matron had laid on my bed. They were always too big or too small for me.

When I reached Spring Park Elementary, I walked past the school building. I was so afraid that the other kids in the classroom would make fun of the black and blue marks on my legs where the head matron had beaten me with the polo paddle. I walked for what seemed to be hours. Finally, I came to this great, big wide street at the end of Spring Park Road. I had never seen one that big before, and I had never seen so many cars in all my life.

Across the street was a big brick store. The sign on top said "Preston's Drugs." There was also a sign in the window that read, "Everything you will ever want is here." It took me almost an hour to get across Atlantic Boulevard, because I was scared of the cars. Finally, I ran across the road as fast as I could, and none of the cars hit me. I walked into the large Preston Drug Store and noticed people sitting at a counter. They had drinks with ice cream in them. I had never seen anything like that before. I do not think I had ever had ice cream, but that is not what I was looking for anyway.

The sign said they had everything that you would ever need in the whole wide world. I had heard about something very special, and I wanted to buy one, if they had it. I looked and I looked and I looked, but I just could not find the thing that I had heard about on the television movie. I was looking around the store when all of a sudden, this old man grabbed me by the arm, and scared the hell out of me.

"What are you doing in here, boy?" he yelled.

"I'm looking for something special," I said as I backed against the wall.

"Are you stealing stuff?"

He pointed directly at my nose.

"No, sir, mister," I said. "I'm not a stealer."

I was directed into a back office, where I was very firmly placed into a hard wooden chair. A police officer came in and asked me why I was not in school. I did not tell him anything, because I was afraid he would take me to jail for running away from the orphanage. Therefore, I started crying very loud. After the police officer left the room, a woman who appeared to be about 25 years old came in and sat by me.

"Were you stealing?" she asked.

"No, ma'am. I was just looking for something special."

"And what might that be?"

"Do you have a hug in this here store?" I asked.

"We always have hugs for kids."

She stood up, wrapped her arms around me, and squeezed very tight. She smiled, and walked out of the small office very fast with her hands over her face. When no one came back for a long time, I looked out the office door and saw that the back door of the store was open. I quickly walked out and ran all the way back to school. When I got there, I found out that I was only about 20 minutes late.

I was the only kid in my class that day that did not have the five-cent milk money for lunch. That was because I had left my nickel on the desk at the Preston Drug Store to pay for the hug that woman gave me. It really was "The store that had everything" in the world that you would ever need; and I didn't have to steal it either.

My First House

All we orphan kids were lined up at the sewing room door. It was another Saturday morning, and anyone who had misbehaved lined up outside the sewing room to receive their punishment. We were made to lie across the sewing table, and then beaten severely with a leather strap. When I use the term beaten, I really mean beaten! In most cases, blood-curdling sounds came from each child. The screams were so intense that the next boy in line would be scared out of his wits when he entered the sewing room door. I will never forget the fear that we orphan boys felt each Saturday morning of our lives, for almost ten years.

"One day he is going to kill one of us," said one of the boys in line.

Nobody had nerve enough to respond to his statement; not even I.

"Next," hollered Mr. Ball, opening the door.

All eyes were upon the boy who was now leaving the sewing room.

"I didn't do nothing wrong," said Bill Smith.

"I don't give a rat's ass if you did or not. Get in here," yelled the house parent, pointing at him.

The door closed, and there was a moment of silence. The first lick with the leather strap came down on Billy, and it came down hard.

"I didn't do nothing, I didn't do nothing," he kept yelling.

However, that made no difference to Mr. Ball. He just kept on beating him. When the beatings were over, we returned to our bedroom until it was time for us to rake the leaves and pine straw. At around noon, we all walked to the shed, took out rakes, and began work on the large yard.

"We got to get out of here before he kills us all," said Wayne Evers.

"They won't kill us. They would go to jail for murder and stuff," I said to the group.

Most of us boys were seven or eight years old at that time. I do not think there has ever been a time in my life that I felt so helpless and defenseless as during that time in the orphanage.

Late that night, five or six of us packed what clothes we could find. Then off we headed; we were going to find us another home to live in. After walking around for hours trying to find an abandoned house, we finally gave up, and walked back to the orphanage gates.

"There is a hole underneath the school building where we could live on our own," said one of the boys.

We boys started walking toward Spring Park Elementary School, which was right next door to the orphanage. Sure enough, there was a crawl space located in the red brick foundation that led under the building.

One at a time, we entered the hole, and found it to be quite spacious. We had to crawl on our hands and knees to get around. It was sandy, it was warm, it was ours, and that was all that mattered to us. This was going to be our new home. For the first time in our lives, we were free. There was no one to beat on us, or to tell us what to do. There were no leaves to rake, or toilets to clean. That was a wonderful, wonderful feeling, even though it was to be short lived.

During the course of the night, we gathered wood for a fire. We used two-by-four studs and old rusty wire to make beds for sleeping, and old apple crates to make dressers. Around three o'clock in the morning, our house was complete.

"Anyone want a smoke?" asked Wayne.

Each of us took a small piece of dried grape vine, and we lit up. There was a cough here and there, but overall it went well. Every boy from the orphanage had already learned to smoke by the age of eight. We sat around the small fire, smoking and looking at our handy work. We called our first meeting to order, and decided we would sneak back over to the orphanage. We needed to gather up several loads of pine straw to use as mattresses. When that was finished, we just sat around looking at our handy work. There were dressers, beds and several bows and arrows, which might be necessary for our protection. We continued to talk with each other, wondering if there was anything else we might possibly need to make our home complete. No one could come up with any additional ideas whatsoever.

"I guess this is it. We have everything we need for a real home," I told the group.

"There is one more thing that we are going to need," said one of the boys.

"And what is that?" asked Wayne.

"Since we have our own house, I guess we're ready for a dog," said Billy Smith.

Every one of us boys just sat there totally dumbfounded, our eyes as big as saucers. Each had a blank look on his face. We had created something that we were not prepared to handle.

It is really a shame when five or six young boys decide to build a home for themselves, and not one of them realizes a woman plays a very important role in the making of a home. Having a "mother" in our lives never even entered our heads.

How It All Begins

My head was still sore where Mrs. Winters, the head matron, had hit me numerous times with her Bible. All I did was ask the Sunday school teacher where babies came from. Ronnie and I were told to go out to the bus until Sunday school was over. I was sent for asking "dumb questions," and Ronnie for laughing. The two of us ran to the bus, and as I started to walk up the small, metal stairs, I stopped.

"You want to run away with me again?" I asked him.

He shrugged his shoulders, and he did not say a word.

"We got money," I told him.

I reached in my pocket, and pulled out the nickel that the orphanage had given me to put in the collection plate. Ronnie reached in his pocket, and he too pulled out a nickel. We smiled, and back down the bus stairs we went. The two of us left the orphanage bus, and headed down some unknown Jacksonville city street.

We walked around for hours looking at the many wonderful things the world outside the orphanage had to offer. As the hours passed, we began to wonder what we were going to do when darkness fell—how we were going to eat, and where we were going to sleep. It was now evening, and more than seven hours had passed since we left Swain Memorial Methodist Church. We were really hungry, and I was cold.

"Maybe we can ask somebody for money. Everyone who lives out here has lots of money. They have nice houses to live in, and real pretty cars," said Ronnie.

"Sir, do you have lots of money?" I asked a passing man.

He stopped, looked at us and then he walked away. All at once, he stopped and tuned around.

"What do you boys need money for?"

"We need to buy food to eat," said Ronnie.

"Where do you boys live?"

I pointed down a side street and just stood there not saying a word.

"Are your parents working?" he asked.

"Yea, they're both at work," I told him.

The man grabbed the two of us by the arm and walked us into a small store several doors down. He grabbed several candy bars from a cardboard box, and two bags of peanuts. We watched him in disbelief, as he went over and paid the clerk. The man handed us each a candy bar and a bag of salted peanuts, patted each of us on the head, and out the door he walked.

"Do you have any money? I sure would like a funny book," yelled Ronnie at another man who came walking into the store.

Sure enough, he talked the man into buying us each a comic book.

"This is great!" I screamed with excitement, as we walked out of the store eating our candy and hugging our free comic book prize.

For several more hours, we walked around asking for money. Here and there we would get a nickel or a dime from a passing stranger. As the hours passed, it got much colder and very windy. The people seemed to disappear, a few at a time. The ones left were ragged, and acted real mean toward us when we asked them for money. Several times, we tried to open car doors. We needed to get inside and warm ourselves, but all of them were locked. Slowly, we made our way to Park Street where we found shelter in the bushes at a local park near Five Points. By now, it was very dark, and we were getting scared.

"Hey, Ronnie. There's a man on that bench over there. Go see if he will give us money for food," I told him.

Without hesitation, he flew out of the bushes, and headed straight for the man. I watched as they talked for more than fifteen minutes. He would sit down on the bench next to the man, and then he would jump up. Then he would sit down again, and then he would jump up again. He kept doing that over and over.

"Come here," I yelled.

He waved at the man, and then began running toward me as fast as he could. When he stopped, he stood there unable to talk. He just stood there breathing very hard.

"Did he give you any money? What did he say?" I questioned.

"He said he'll give us money so we can eat, if I wiggle his thing back and forth."

"What thing?"

"The thing he uses the bathroom with."

"Why can't he wiggle it all by himself and still give us some money?" I whispered to little Ronnie.

"He won't. I done asked him."

"Well, I ain't going to touch nobody's thing. That's a nasty thing."

"I know, but we gotta get some nickels and dimes," Ronnie said.

"What you want to do?"

"Well, it ain't a real big deal."

"What ain't a big deal?"

"His thing, it ain't real big, and it's all wrinkly like. He showed it to me with his matches. I seen it."

"Are you going to touch it for money?" I asked.

"You want me to?"

"I don't think we should do something bad like that. Do you?" I said.

"I'm going to ask him how much he's gonna give us, okay?"

Once again, Ronnie was gone in a flash. I had just turned eight, and he was a much faster runner than I was. Boy could that six-year-old kid run. I lay there in the shadows, watching them by the little bit of moonlight that would appear now and then as the clouds moved slowly overhead. I waited and I waited and I waited. The two of them talked for what seemed to be half the night.

"Roger!" screamed Ronnie.

I jumped when I heard his voice. I had fallen asleep, and was confused, and did not know where I was.

"Roger! He's hurting me!" I heard again.

I jumped up and ran as fast as I could toward the park bench. As I came to a sliding stop on the sidewalk, I saw that the man was forcing Ronnie's head into his lap.

"I'm going to call Mother Winters," I yelled at the man.

The man did not stop what he was doing. I could hear Ronnie choking and trying to breathe. I pushed the back of the park bench as hard as I could. The bench fell over backwards, spilling the man and Ronnie onto the ground. Ronnie jumped up and began running down the sidewalk toward the bushes. When I looked down, I saw the man's pants lying at my feet. I grabbed his pants and off I ran to catch up with Ronnie.

"Run, Ronnie, run!" I yelled at him as I passed him by.

The two of us ran for what seemed to be miles before we stopped. He and I stood shivering behind the old, red, brick church, and tried to rest. I took the man's pants, and I wrapped them around Ronnie to keep him warm. He and I fell asleep, and did not wake up until early the next morning.

After we got ourselves together, we headed down the street to who-knows-where. Still carrying the man's pants, I began wadding them in a ball so that I could throw them in a garbage can that we saw ahead of us. All at once, I felt a hard knot. I stopped and rolled the pants out onto the ground. In the back pocket, I found a billfold. Ronnie watched as I opened the wallet and looked inside.

"There must be a million dollars in there!" screamed Ronnie.

I could not believe my eyes as I looked at row after row after row of green dollar bills. Ronnie was jumping all over the place. After calming him down, I put the wallet inside my shirt, picked up the pants, and threw them into the garbage can. Several blocks down the street, I saw a big metal mailbox. I took the money out of the billfold and stuck it in my front pocket. I threw the man's wallet in the mail slot, and off we walked. Several blocks later, we decided to go into a restaurant and buy something to eat. Ronnie and I sat down at the table, and waited to be served.

"Can I help you, gentlemen?" asked the waitress.

"We want lots of food, and we don't want no eggplant or okra, like at the orphanage," said Ronnie.

The waitress stood there looking a little puzzled.

"Tell me what you want," she said, with a disgusted look on her face.

"I would like to have some coffee, like Mother Winters has. And lots of sugar, too," I replied.

"Aren't you too young for coffee?" she inquired.

"I got money. Lots of money."

I reached into my pocket and laid the large stack of bills on the tabletop.

"I want to eat everything on that page, right there," Ronnie told her, as he pointed to the food items shown on the back of the menu.

The waitress dropped her hands to her sides, turned around and walked into the kitchen. Several minutes later, a large man dressed in a dirty, white uniform came walking toward us.

"What do you boys want?"

"I want all the food on that page, right there," Ronnie told him.

"Where did you boys get all that money," the cook asked, as he pointed at the large bills.

"My dad is rich. He's real rich," I said in a very authoritative voice.

"Yeah, just because we live in the orphanage doesn't mean we can't be rich," yelled Ronnie.

The man said not a word. He turned around and walked away. I was surprised when the waitress returned, bringing each of us a cup of coffee.

"And lots of sugar!" hollered Ronnie.

The waitress turned around and walked back down the aisle, shaking her head the entire time. The two of us ate until we could eat no more. We had no idea that such wonderful foods even existed on the face of this earth. The two of us sat there for almost an hour, laughing and drinking coffee.

I looked up at Ronnie and I asked, "Did you ever touch that man's thing?"

When I looked up, the waitress was looking directly at me.

"Let me have those two whole pies, and put them in a bag," Ronnie instructed the woman, as he pointed at the glass case located on the end of the counter.

The woman just stood there, continually staring at me.

"Joe, call the police," said the waitress.

The cook walked over, picked up the black telephone and began dialing. I picked up the money and I handed the woman a $20 bill.

Slowly, she backed up to the cash register and made it open. When she looked away, I slid part of the money off the table, folded it in half and stuck it in my sock.

Several minutes later, the police arrived and questioned us for more than fifteen minutes. Neither of us would say who we were or where we were from.

When the police officers asked us to stand up, I reached out and picked up the remaining money off the table. The officer quickly reached out and took it from my hand. As the two of us were marched down the aisle of the restaurant, Ronnie was yelling, "I want my two pies in a bag. I want my two pies."

As I passed the waitress, I stuck my tongue out at her. She in return, did the same thing to me.

The "N" Word

Having spent my entire childhood in a Jacksonville, Florida orphanage, we kids never knew about the prejudices known to the rest of the world. At least, we did not think that we were prejudiced. I remember running away from the orphanage when I was about eight years old. I was walking down Riverside Avenue, when I happened to duck behind a restaurant. I had seen a police car driving toward me. Standing by the back door of the restaurant was a young Negro boy about my same age. A large white man was handing the young boy a paper bag. He rubbed the little boy on top of his head, and then he closed the door. The little boy reached into the paper bag, pulled out a chicken leg and began to eat it, as if he were starving.

"You like chicken legs?" asked the boy, looking up at me with his big white eyes.

"I guess."

I had not eaten since very early that same morning, and I did not have any money.

"Here!"

He held the paper bag open to me. I reached in, took out a chicken leg and began to eat it.

"You want to walk down to my house with me?" asked the boy.

"Sure," I told him.

We walked out onto Riverside Avenue and headed toward the park. It was the park where I always stayed when I ran away from the orphanage.

"Get off the road, nigger boy," yelled someone from a vehicle driving past us at a high rate of speed.

I looked up to see who had yelled, but I did not know them. The Negro boy did not say a word. He just kept on eating his chicken leg and walking. Less than a block down the road, the same car came past us again.

"You like walking with niggers, boy?"

There was a white boy hanging halfway out of the passenger window yelling.

"Don't say anything. Just keep on walking," said the Negro boy.

"Why would they call me a nigger like that?" I asked the boy.

"They ain't talking to you. They talkin' to me."

"No, they are talking to me," I said.

"You ain't black. You can't be no nigger."

"The orphanage always calls us kids niggers. How would those guys know that I am from the orphanage?" I questioned.

"You got to be black to be called a real nigger," he explained

"Black… black like a black crayon? Is a black crayon called a nigger?" I asked.

"No. That is different. You gotta be a Negro person to be called a nigger."

"That doesn't make any sense at all to me. I ain't black, so why does the orphanage call me a nigger?" I asked.

"I don't know why they do that," he responded.

We walked about a block before the car came around once again.

"What you got in that damn bag, boy?" hollered one of the people in the car.

"Just chicken legs," I told him.

The Negro boy wrapped the bag into a ball, and held it tight to his chest.

"Bring me the damn bag!" yelled the man driving the car.

We just stood there too afraid to move. All of a sudden, the car door opened and one of the boys stepped out onto the sidewalk.

"Give me that bag right now," he said.

He was shaking a small hammer that was in his hand. The Negro boy held out the bag and let it drop to the ground. He and I took off running as fast as we could across the street and into the park. We stopped by a large tree and looked back to see what was happening. The boy with the hammer had picked up the brown paper bag and was dumping the contents all over the sidewalk. The man and two other boys had exited the car, and all four began laughing and stomping on the chicken. After they kicked the chicken off the sidewalk, they got back in the car and they drove away.

I walked the boy back to his house, where I met his mom and dad. As we sat on their front porch drinking iced tea, I waited for him to tell them about what happened, but he never did. He acted as though being called a "nigger" was just a normal, everyday thing. I will remember that incident for as long as I live. I will never forget the look I saw in his eyes or the scared look I saw on his face. However, more than that, I will never forget what it feels like to be called a "nigger," no matter what color you are.

I Won't Be Back For Many a Day

It is a very scary thing for a young boy to be heading out into the world on his own, especially when he has been a prisoner in an orphanage most of his young life. Though I was only eight years old, I still had many smarts about myself—at least enough smarts to try to survive on my own on the streets of Jacksonville, Florida. I was somewhat withdrawn, but I was a very aware little boy. I had learned very early in life what adults were capable of doing to young boys and girls, if they did not do exactly as they are told.

Out the second-story window of the boy's dormitory I went. I quietly slid along the roof on my rear end, making my way over to the large oak tree at the end of the porch and then climbed down to the ground. I tiptoed along the porch until I got to the azalea bushes, and then ran as fast as I could toward the large, white gates at the entrance of the orphanage. It was rather cold, and I was quite scared. This was the very first time I had run away from the orphanage all by myself. I had no money, no food, and nowhere to go. However, all that really mattered to me now was getting away from the beating and abuse that we children had to suffer, almost on a daily basis.

I stopped at the front gates and turned around to see if anybody was coming after me. Luckily, no one was coming. I just stood there in the dark for a moment. I was remembering a song that I had heard that evening on the Ed Sullivan Show. Some black man named "Harry" somebody or something like that was singing: "Sad to say, I'm on my way. Won't be back for many a day. Da da da and da da da. I'm going down to Kingston town." I stood there for a moment singing that song very softly to myself. The song told me that there was a good place for me somewhere in the world—a place that was far, far away from this orphanage.

I stood silently watching as the cars drove past. I stooped down, hiding myself in the dark shadows of the pine trees and bushes that surrounded the front gates of the orphanage. The cold wind from the passing cars was hitting me, making me shiver as they passed. Bravely, I pulled myself together and walked out the gates, and down Spring Park Road. I was heading out into a world that I knew absolutely nothing about, for the very first time. I walked for what seemed to be hours before I came to a large, metal bridge that was painted silver.

"The Main Street Bridge," I said aloud to myself.

I raised my shirt collar and stuck my little hands in my pockets to keep myself warm. I leaned forward, placing one foot in front of the other, and I began walking up the steep incline of the bridge. Huffing and puffing, I made my way to the center portion of the bridge before I stopped. I raised my head and looked around at the beautiful city of Jacksonville. Oh, what a beautiful site it was to see thousands upon thousands of lights way off in the darkness. To see for the first time in my life, hundreds upon hundreds of brightly lit red lights on the back of cars as they exited from the large bridge. I looked at the faces of the people in the cars as they passed me by. Not one of them even realized that I was standing there. Now it was just myself, scared, and all alone.

"Being out here in the world is no different than being in the orphanage," I thought to myself. "There's really nobody in the whole wide world that really cares about me. They don't even know that I'm alive."

I sat down on the sidewalk of the bridge, and began to cry.

"Are you okay?" asked a strange voice, coming from behind me.

I jumped up, placed my back against the metal railing of the bridge, and stood there shaking.

"Are you okay?" the man asked again.

"Yes, sir. I'm just a little bit cold and tired, sir." I told him.

"Let's get off this cold bridge, and go somewhere that is warm," said the man.

We walked for several miles talking with each another. Then we walked into a little coffee shop restaurant, where the man bought me a hamburger and a Coke. He told me that he was a schoolteacher, and that I should not be out on the streets alone at night. It was very dangerous, especially for young kids. While we were eating, I told him that I was from the orphanage, and that I had run away because they beat us all the time.

He invited me to come to his apartment for the night so that we could talk and be friends. He even let me take a good hot bath in a real bathtub, for the very first time in my life. Then he told me that I could spend the night. We said a prayer together, and I asked God if I could stay and live with him forever and ever. After I had fallen asleep, I suddenly awoke when I felt the bed jerk. There was my friend Bill standing at the foot of the bed. He had no clothes on whatsoever.

He made me promise him on my heart that I would never tell anyone about what he did to me that night. After he went to sleep, I got up very quietly and dressed myself. Then I snuck out of the apartment house. In the cold and the darkness, I walked back across the great big, metal bridge and back into the gates of the orphanage. I stopped for just a moment, and started to cry. I turned around and looked back at the outside world through the orphanage fence. Softly, I started singing to myself: "Sad to say, I'm on my way. Won't be back for many a day. Da da da and da da da. I'm never going back to Kingston town."

The Wire Cage

I closely watched everyone and everything that was happening around me. I constantly shifted my eyes from right to left and left to right, while looking into the eyes and faces of the adults who were discussing what they should do with me. I watched the large stacks of paperwork as they were shuffled from desk to desk, and from person to person.

My little eight-year-old heart would jump inside my chest every time that hollow sound would come rushing down the dark hallways. It was a sound made, as one of the many large steel doors was being slammed shut. Almost in a comatose state, I would sit motionless. I would stare straight ahead, nervously fumbling with my fingers, and silently watching as telephone after telephone rang. All these big ol' mean-looking people wearing suits and ties answered the calls.

I sat for hours and watched, as police officer after police officer walked past me. Not one of them paid any attention to the fact that I was a living, breathing little boy. I was just a little bitty human being, living and trying to find himself a place on this mean old earth.

"Come with me," someone would say, rather sternly. I would be transferred from one chair to another, as more and more paper work was being completed.

"Tap, tap, tap," would go the typewriters.

"Ring, ring," would sound the telephones.

"Hello, may I help you?"

"Good bye."

"That is correct."

"No. The judge is not in at the moment."

"Yes."

"That is not my problem."

Those were the sounds of the hundreds of thousands of words being thrown around the office where I sat. Just like all the other times that I had run away from the orphanage, I knew that it was just a matter of time before I would once again be locked away. A firm, coarse hand on my shoulder, and another in the middle of my back would lead me out of this scary office. My tiny little legs would march as fast as they could down the dimly lit hallway to the waiting elevator, be taken upstairs to the juvenile hall, and locked away in one of the many wire cages.

Oh, how wonderful it felt to finally be locked away, all by myself in a dark, cold steel wire cage—to finally be alone, so that I could curl up into a ball on the hard, steel bed without anyone seeing me, to let my little body go limp and feel all the pain, fear and fright come floating out of me from deep inside. A time for me to be alone without anyone laughing or thinking I was a weak little boy who could not stand on his own two feet.

"I see that you are back with us once again," said a gruff-sounding voice standing in the shadows.

"Yes, sir," I replied, as I looked up and saw the shadow of one of the juvenile counselors.

"It's sort of scary, isn't it?" he asked me.

"Kind of," I told him, in a low voice.

He opened the door to the wire cage, walked over, sat down beside me, and placed his arm around my neck.

"Do you feel like you want to cry sometimes?"

"No, sir. Just kind of scared," I said.

"Sometimes it's good to cry," he said in a low whisper.

"Do you ever cry?" I asked.

"Sometimes," he replied.

"Why would someone cry when you are not being spanked or something like that?" I asked with my eyes opening very wide.

"Roger. Don't you ever cry just because you feel hurt or feel bad inside?" he questioned, with a puzzled look on his face.

"Why would someone cry, if they are not getting beat on? That don't make any sense," I said.

"Haven't you ever cried because you don't have a mother and father?"

"No," I said.

"What about having to live in the orphanage? Isn't that sad?"

"I guess that is sort of sad. We have to work all the time," I replied.

"Don't you kids ever get to play at the orphanage?"

"Sure we do. When the matron's not looking, we play cowboys and Indians with the broom and rake handle," I blurted out, smiling from ear to ear.

He smiled, patted me on the back, and got up from the steel bunk.

"Would you like to work here at the shelter?"

"Sure," I said. "I'm a good worker too. I can clean toilets and wash floors better than anybody washes. Nobody I know can wax floors better than me."

"Young man, would you like a hug?"

"I guess," I responded shrugging my shoulders.

The counselor stood in front of me and placed his arms around my shoulders. He squeezed very tight like. It felt kind of weird and funny. Then he let go of me, walked out of the door of the cage, and locked it with his key.

"Let me see what I can do about making you a worker in the office," he said with a smile on his face. He raised his hand and waved at me. Then he turned and walked away.

I heard the outer steel door close and then lock, and I listened with my ear against the wire as his steps disappeared in the distance. I stood in the corner for the longest time thinking about the hug that the counselor had given me. I had only been hugged once before, and that was by a man who came to the orphanage on Easter Morning to hide eggs for all the orphan children. He hugged me in the bathroom, and then made me take all my clothes off, and he lay on top of me.

I curled up in a tight ball on the steel bunk, and could feel water running out of my eyes. I knew that it was just a matter of time before the counselor would come back. He would hug me again, make me take my clothes off, and he would lie on top of me, as the "Easter Egg Man" had done. However, that never did happen, even though the counselor did hug me many, many times over the next couple of months. He was always very kind to me, and he never hurt me.

I now look back as a grown man, through the many relationships that I have had with numerous women throughout the years. I wonder if I could possibly count all the times that I secretly wondered if I would have to take my clothes off, just because I allowed them to hug me.

Running To
Who-Knows-Where

As I look back on one particular night, I remember us boys from the Children's Home Society, all ranging in ages from eight to twelve. We were cold and a little bit hungry as we walked the darkened streets of Jacksonville. This was one of many times that we had run away from the orphanage for no particular reason. Maybe because we were hungry. Maybe one of us had been beaten or molested by the matron. Who knows? I guess there comes a time in every young life when inexperienced "buzzards" have to spread their wings and venture out into the unknown.

I remember the cold breeze hitting us in the face, as the speeding cars would pass us by. We walked hunched over with our hands in our pockets and our shoulders shrugged up around our necks, trying to stay as warm as possible. We stopped for a moment to rest after making it to the South Gate Plaza Shopping Mall on Atlantic Boulevard. We stood watching as families walked out of the stores carrying armloads of Christmas gifts to their cars. We were motionless as we stood and watched, and we didn't say one word. We watched as little children and their parents laughed and played with each other. We could hardly believe all the gifts that they were loading into their cars.

"It's Christmas time in the city," sang one of the boys in a low whisper. "Ding-a-ling," he continued to sing very softly.

"Shut up!" said one of the other boys, as he turned around and pushed the boy in the middle of his chest.

"It's just a Christmas song," said the young boy.

"Just shut up!" I said.

We stood there silently looking at the thousands upon thousands of red, green, yellow and blue Christmas lights that decorated the outside of the Southgate Plaza Shopping Center. Not one of us said a word as family after family came out of the shopping mall. We just watched as other children ran around laughing and playing.

"Go ahead and sing that song anyway," said the older boy.

"Silver bells, silver bells. It's Christmas time in the city," sang the young boy. "Ding-a-ling, ding-a-ling, silver bells, silver bells, make 'em ring. It's Christmas time in the city."

I looked around at each of the boys in our group. The Christmas lights reflected off the wet cheeks of one of them. I am not sure what was going through the minds of the other boys as we stood there. I do know that it made me sad to see all those little kids laughing and being hugged—lucky little kids who had their very own mothers and fathers, not to mention all those presents. To know that shortly they would soon be warm in their very own house, where they had their very own room, and their very own toys.

Suddenly, the silence was broken as a man yelled out, "Get your damn ass in that car and keep your damn mouth shut."

The man shoved the woman against the side of a car. When the woman hit the car, she slid down to the ground. The little girl ran over to her mother, and she started to cry.

"You shut your mouth, too. Get your little butt in the back seat of the car," he demanded.

He jerked the little girl up by the arm. All at once, he reached over and slapped the girl across her back as hard as he could. We boys just stood there, too afraid to move a muscle.

"Get your ass up and get in the damn car," he yelled at the woman.

Slowly, she got to her feet, and walked around to the other side of the car.

"I said get in the damn car," he yelled at her again pointing at her.

She opened the car door, and sat down in the seat. The man stepped into the car and closed his door. For several minutes, they just sat there. He continued to yell and scream at her. However, we could not understand what it was that he was saying. All at once, he reached over and slapped the woman across the face, and then he grabbed her around the throat.

"Hey, mister! You ain't supposed to hit no woman like that," yelled the older boy with us.

The man let go of the woman, put the car in gear and squealed his tires as he left the parking lot. We boys just stood there looking at each other. No one said a word as we walked back into the gates of the orphanage. We knew that there was nothing for us inside that place. Therefore, whatever goodness was to be found in the world, it had to be found outside the gates of the orphanage itself. Seeing that man knock that woman to the ground, then slap his little girl across her back, made us aware that the world outside the orphanage was not as kind, friendly and loving as we had thought.

There were many more times that we boys ran away from the orphanage. However, running away never was the same to us after that. There was nothing "good" for us to search for anymore. Now when we ran away, we really did not have a place to run, so we just started running to "who-knows-where."

In The Patio

It was hotter than hot in the orphanage, and we could not sleep. It was almost as if someone had thrown a hot, wet blanket over you, and it was very hard to breathe. However, that was just part of the problem. One of the boys had dropped the soap sock down the toilet, it had run over and water was all over the bathroom floor. Therefore, we all had to clean it up, and go to bed without any supper.

I was exceptionally hungry, and had not eaten anything since breakfast. That morning, I had thrown my school lunch away, because we kids had to carry it in a brown paper bag, and that was a sign that you were from the orphanage. I did not want anyone at school to know that I lived at the orphanage.

About ten of us decided to sneak out my bedroom window, and head out into the unknown world—the world outside of the orphanage fences. We had heard they threw away lots of good food at Morrison's Restaurant Cafeteria at the South Gate Plaza Shopping Center.

Therefore, off went our little herd of orphans, heading out into the world in search of food and drink.

As we walked toward the shopping center, we passed a building called the Patio Restaurant. The establishment, now closed for a few hours, still had the smell of cooked food coming from the back window. It drew us like bees to honey. We walked around and around the building, trying to find out where that delicious smell was coming from. Several of the boys were looking through the garbage cans. Robert noticed the back window was slightly open, and called for us to come over. That wonderful smell was being blown through the back window by a large fan on the kitchen.

As we stood in line taking turns smelling the wonderful aroma coming from the restaurant, one of the boys leaned against the lower pane of glass and it slid out of its metal case. Of course, it did not take us long to figure out that the other plates of glass would also slide out. One after the other, we removed the glass carefully placing them beside the back door. Within minutes, all ten of us were standing inside eating candy, pie and cake. We had never eaten like this before in our entire lives. It was like being in candy heaven. After we had eaten all we wanted, we cleaned up after ourselves, and went back out through the back window. We replaced the glass and returned to the orphanage for a good night's sleep.

All the next day, we talked about what we had done. Finding a candy heaven was the greatest thing that could ever happen to us. We boys agreed that we would return every night. We'd eat what we wanted, clean up our mess, and then leave, so no one would be the wiser. We felt no one would be hurt or injured by what we were doing, as long as we did not damage or break anything. This worked out rather well for the first few days, but then some of the boys talked about taking cigarettes and matches. Most of us were against it, because that was stealing. Eating food was okay, because this was America, and everybody should have the right to eat food and be full.

I would guess we ended up taking about ten cartons of Parliaments, with the recessed filter. That was the first cigarette I ever smoked. It is unbelievable how a cigarette hanging in the mouth of a nine-year-old can make the girls forget your big elephant ears. However, eventually you will run out of cigarettes, and then your ears seem to get big all over again, all of a sudden.

About three weeks later, Wayne Evers and I decided to return to the Patio Restaurant to get another few cartons of cigarettes. When we got to the restaurant, I helped Wayne into the window, because he was too small to reach the window ledge. After he climbed inside the building, I also climbed in, and ran to get several cartons of cigarettes. I was the first one to go back out the window, so I could help Wayne get back out, and down to the ground again. As my feet hit the ground, I ran quickly over to the bushes to hide my cigarettes. Just at that moment, I noticed a police car coming around the corner toward the back of the restaurant. I lay down very quickly in the bushes, and watched as the police officer got out of his car. He walked very slowly up to Wayne, who was sliding backward out of the window. The police officer, saying not a word, began helping Wayne out of the window.

"Don't pull on me, Roger," Wayne yelled.

The police officer did not say a word; he just kept pulling on Wayne. Once again, Wayne began yelling at me not to pull so hard. Then he began kicking his legs. All at once, he fell out of the window landing on his stomach.

"You dumb turd," he hollered.

When he stood up, he finally saw the police officer standing behind him! I did not see Wayne for about two or three days. They finally did bring him back to the orphanage, after he got out of the juvenile court for "being a thief." I gave him just a few cigarettes out of my two cartons of Parliaments. I did not want to run out of cigarettes, and have the girls tell me my ears had gotten big again, at least not any sooner than was necessary.

Was my running away the reason I began to smoke, and the reason I continue to smoke cigarettes, even today? Was my running away the reason I learned to steal, and became a thief for many years? When we are cold, hungry and lonely, we will do whatever is necessary to survive. Our minds begin to tell us that we are justified in doing whatever is necessary to take care of and protect ourselves.

It does not take long before stealing, lying, cheating, and even selling ourselves becomes a normal everyday thing. It becomes a life that has no feelings of guilt. Once you make the decision, as a child, to do adult things to protect yourself, you can never be a kid again. Not ever!

There Is Something Wrong With Me

"Stand up and face the judge," said the court officer, as he motioned at us boys with his hand.

All five of us boys, ranging in ages from eight to eleven, stood up and faced the judge's bench.

"This is not the first time many of you boys have stood before me. I doubt it will be the last," he told us.

We just stood there looking down at the floor.

"What was there to be afraid of?" I thought to myself. "What can a judge do to us that the orphanage was not already doing?

"Boy, that judge sure has a big head for a human. That's the biggest head I've ever seen," I continued thinking to myself.

"Are you listening to me, boy?" screamed Judge Gooding.

I looked up from the floor, and saw that he was staring directly at me. I just stood there staring back at him. I did not know what it was that he wanted me to say.

"Bring that boy to my chambers," instructed the judge as he stood up.

The court officer put his hand into the middle of my back, and pushed me along. As I walked, I looked back to see what Robert, Wayne, Eugene and Billy were doing. They were just standing there with scared looks on their faces.

"Have a seat right there," said the judge, as he pointed at a chair sitting beside his large desk.

I took a seat, and sat there waiting for him to speak.

"What seems to be your problem?" the judge asked me.

"I don't have any problems," I told him, as I sat there with my hands folded on my lap.

"This is a very serious charge. Breaking and entering into the Patio Restaurant—it's very serious indeed."

"We didn't break anything."

He just sat there shaking his big head back and forth.

"Then why did you fellows break into that restaurant?" he asked.

"We were hungry. We saw candy bars through the window, so we took out the glass on the back side, went in and started eating all the candy bars."

"Don't you understand that breaking and entering is wrong—that you boys violated the law?" he continued, as he pushed his large head toward me.

"But we were hungry."

"Look, boy. If I am going to help you, you have to meet me half way. We both have to give a little."

"What do you want me to give? I live at the orphanage, and I don't have anything to give."

"Is that all that you have to say?" the judge questioned.

"You sure got a big head. How come you got such a big head like that?" I said.

"What's wrong with you, boy?" He yelled at me.

"I don't know. I think there is something wrong with me inside my head. That is what the orphanage says all the time. But I don't know what they mean."

"It is your big mouth. You do not know when to keep it shut. That's the main part of your problem."

"The orphanage told me that there's something wrong with me deep down inside my head," I muttered.

"Do you think that you are like all the other children who live at the orphanage?

"I guess. I seem just like the rest of them. I do not see anything wrong with me. I do what every body else does."

"Are you telling me that you do not know the difference between right and wrong?

"I know the difference between right and wrong," I said.

"Then why did you boys break into that restaurant last night?"

"'Cause we was hungry." I told him for the second time.

"If it was wrong, then why did you choose to do it?"

"Now I'm getting confused, like I don't know what you mean."

"Do you have any plans for your life?" asked Judge Gooding.

"I plan to have my own good food to eat one day."

"Maybe ten days in lock-up will help you get un-confused," he told me as he pointed toward the ceiling where the juvenile lock-up was located.

"What about the other boys?" I questioned.

"Don't you worry about those other boys. I'll take care of them."

"But they ate the candy bars, too, just like me."

The five of us were locked up in a detention cell in the Duval County Juvenile Hall for ten days. A week later, we were taken back to the Children's Home Society Orphanage. For years, I was very confused about what Judge Marion Gooding had said to me that day in his courtroom. For years, I kept silent about my past, as well as my life in the orphanage. For years, I always wondered what was wrong with me. I have always wondered what it was that they saw in me. Why was I different from other children?

As I look back, I can see that stealing those candy bars was, without a doubt, the wrong thing to do. However, we boys were hungry. Getting to that candy was not a matter of right or wrong. It was a matter of instinct and survival. I hope that things have changed for the children of today. I hope that parents are smart enough to take the time to try to understand what it is that makes a child do and act a certain way, before giving up on them.

When I turned 29 years old, I secretly went to see a psychiatrist and I had him test me. For two weeks, I underwent every test known to the doctor. My IQ was a little above the normal range, and I was about average in all other aspects of the tests. It is amazing to me when I look back and see the damage that intelligent, civilized adults have done to the children of the past.

Totally In The Dark

"You are about as worthless as they come," said the judge, as I stood there before him.

I just stood motionless with my head down, staring at the floor, and not knowing what to say. Besides, what does any nine-year-old boy say when he does not have the slightest idea what all these grown up people are talking about anyway.

"Not only that, but I think you have grave psychological problems. What is your problem?" he continued.

"I know what those words mean, 'cause I've been told that many times before," I thought to myself.

The part that I could not understand is why all the grown up people that I know at the orphanage think that I am different from all the other kids.

"It's true that I get into a lot of trouble when I climb trees and build army forts under the ground, stuff like that. But so do the other kids," I said to myself, as the judge carried on and on.

"What is your problem?" yelled the judge at the top of his voice.

"I don't know, sir," I replied.

"Maybe two weeks in the Juvenile Shelter will teach you a thing or two," he stated.

"What is it that he wants from me? What is it that I am supposed to say to him, to let him know I understand what he is talking about?" I thought to myself.

I looked about the courtroom, and I saw the juvenile detention officer looking directly at me. Then there was the clerk of the court, and the woman who was writing everything down. Mrs. Winters, the head matron, was also looking at me with a smirk on her face, and no one was saying anything at all.

"I don't know, your judge, sir," I said.

"You don't know what?" asked the Judge.

"I don't know what you mean," I stated.

My little mind was racing fifty thousand miles per hour in my head. I was so scared, and had no idea what everyone was talking about.

"I wish they would tell me what is wrong with me. I wish someone would take the time to tell me what it is about me that makes others think I am not right in my head," I thought to myself.

"Stop playing with your fingers," said the judge, as he pointed at me.

I lowered my hands to my sides and stood there, all alone, all afraid and all scared like. My little mind just became a total blank, and I fell to the floor. The next thing I remember, I was once again locked inside the wire cage, which was located upstairs in the Juvenile Court Hall building.

As I sit here writing this story, 46 years later, I now understand somewhat what was happening to me, as well as what the problem might have been—and continued to be—for me for many, many years. Even to this day, I am not exactly sure what it is (or was) that they were talking about, that I was supposed to be doing wrong.

As a little boy, I may have very well had "psychological problems." However, I certainly did not realize that a problem even existed. How could I? I was only nine years old. To me, I appeared to be completely normal.

The problem, as I see it now, was loneliness, sadness, distrust and depression. As a little boy in the orphanage home, I did not even know what such things were. If I felt sad, lonely and distrustful or depressed, those were just normal feelings to me. How would any nine-year-old boy know other people were not feeling exactly the same type of feelings that he was? How would he know that feelings like those were not normal, and that they were making him not only feel, but act differently from others his same age?

Had I been smart or intelligent enough to know about such things at that young age, what could I have done about it anyway? Any mistakes made in my case were made by the adults, as far as I am concerned. Grown adults concluding that a nine-year-old boy knew what he was doing, why he was doing it, and expecting him to understand why he felt as he did, is a crazy way of thinking. Expecting a young boy to know and understand the answer to those questions is preposterous.

I am very upset that I was sent to a reform school just because I ran away from the orphanage. I am very upset that these adults made a decision in my life that started a process that led me from orphanage to reform school, from reform school to jail, and eventually to prison. There is no doubt that I helped get myself into these types of institutions. Let there be no doubt that I knew the difference between right and wrong.

However, I can honestly say it was the adults that gave up on me. No one in authority would listen when I tried to tell them I was forced to eat human waste, made to drink urine, hung by my neck in a tree, burnt on a stove, and made to take off my clothes so adults could lay on top of me. These are the people who failed, not I.

I walked out of prison on February 6, 1969, at 24 years of age. That was the very first day in my life when I could say and do whatever I pleased. I have never been in trouble again.

Stealing

"Don't you know that it is wrong to steal?" asked the woman.

"Yes, ma'am," I answered.

"Then why do you steal, if you know it is wrong?"

I stood there trying to find an answer that I knew would satisfy her.

"I steal because that's the way it's done."

"What do you mean?" she questioned.

"If you need food, and you do not got no job, then you just have to steal food."

"That's not true, and you know it."

"But I don't know what you mean," I said.

"Don't you know that stealing is wrong?" she asked again.

"I know that it's wrong, but what else is there to do?"

"You really do not know, do you?" she responded.

I was nine or ten years old when that conversation occurred. Now that I am 57 years old, I can look back and see exactly what it was that she was talking about.

However, at the time, I was a very confused little boy. When running away from the orphanage, we boys would not eat for a day or two at a time. As a last resort, we would walk into a store, and steal bread and meat for sandwiches. This went on for years. So long, in fact, that it became commonplace for us to steal. Stealing became a necessity of life. Stealing was just as normal to us as was the sun coming up each morning.

The point here is that each one of us knew that stealing was wrong. There was no doubt about that.

"But what other way is there to have stuff like other kids have?" we would ask ourselves.

In order for children not to steal, there must be a negative feeling associated with the act of stealing—some type of feeling that makes one feel guilty when he steals something that does not belong to him. We boys were running the streets as if we were a pack of wild, hungry dogs searching for prey. Stealing to us was nothing more than survival. When caught, we were taken before the juvenile court. We knew that we had done something wrong. We also knew that there was a price to be paid.

Many times, we told Judge Gooding that we were stealing food because we were going hungry. He would call us liars. He would roll his eyes into the back of his head, and then lock us up in juvenile hall. However, after that was over, we were right back where we started in the first place—back to being hungry and mistreated. We were hungry, we were scared, and we did not have the slightest idea where to turn, except to stealing. We knew that stealing would feed us, and that stealing was our only option.

Not once did we ever feel guilty about what we were doing. That was the worst part of the entire mess. Many of the boys, and many of the girls, continued to steal for years. All the while knowing that it was legally wrong, but no one ever seemed to feel guilty about it. Feeling guilty never crossed our little minds, even for an instant. Steal and get caught, steal and get caught, steal and get caught. It became a never-ending cycle.

Those were the terms of the act of stealing. There was never anyone to tell us that there were other options open to us. In fact, there were no other options, other than going hungry. Telling a child that stealing food is wrong when he is hungry has very little meaning. As a child, I sat on the beach many a night eating raw hamburger, which we had stolen from a grocery store. We boys all sat in a circle, shivering from the cold. And we had blood all over our faces from eating raw meat, as if we were wild animals.

The Tank

"Strip 'em down and put them in the drunk tank." The fat police sergeant sitting behind the desk was shouting demands.

All five of us kids were stripped down to our underwear and placed inside a tiled room. The room was bare of anything, except for a tiled bench seat that ran completely around the room. The temperature was very cold; it must have been somewhere around 40 degrees. Generally, when we boys ran away from the orphanage, we were taken to the juvenile hall located on Market Street. From what I could gather from the officer's conversation, the juvenile hall was full. Therefore, we were to be taken to the Duval County jail, until other arrangements could be made.

We ranged in age from nine to ten years of age. We sat there with our hands folded between our legs trying to stay as warm as possible. No matter what position you would find, you just could not get warm. Every half hour or so, the big steel door would open, and another drunken adult would be pushed inside. They would stagger around for several minutes mumbling to themselves, and then lay down on the floor and go to sleep. Occasionally, one of the men would wake up and start to throw up all over the floor. As the hours passed, the smell became more and more intolerable. It became so horrible that several of us started to get sick and throw up, too. I would constantly bang on the steel door asking the guards to move us to another cell that did not smell.

Finally, in order to keep warm, we huddled in a group with our backs to each other. Just as we were about to get some warmth, we heard the steel door unlock and swing open. Two jail guards came rushing in holding a large fire hose. They immediately began spraying everyone down with cold water. Everyone in the cell began to yell and scream at the top of his voice.

That had to be one of the worst nights of my life. I was ten years old at that time. As I sat in the corner of the large, cold cell shivering, I wondered how people could treat other human beings with such cruelty. I can remember being totally confused. Even at that young age, I could understand people being mean to one another, but only if they were being threatened. However, to make someone almost freeze to death and then laugh about it was very confusing to me.

Hour after hour, we sat there freezing in that jail cell. Several of the boys started to cry, and said that their ears hurt them. I felt like crying myself, but by the age of ten, I had already become very hard inside. There was no way I was going to let anyone see me cry, and there was no way I was going to beg for mercy. Most of us had already been up for about 30 hours and just as I was about to fall asleep, the steel door opened once again. Standing in the doorway was a big man with his hands on his hips.

"What are these kids doing in here?" he questioned one of the guards standing behind him.

"Don't really know, sir. They were brought in on the last shift."

"Get these kids some damn blankets. They're freezing to death!" said the large man.

"Yes, sir," said the guard, as he turned and headed down the long hallway.

"You kids ate anything?" asked the man.

"Not since yesterday morning," said one of the boys.

"You boys get up and get out here in the hallway."

He pointed at us one at a time. One by one, we made our way to the door. As we exited, a wool blanket was wrapped around each of us. We sat in a line on the floor in the hallway and each of us was given a cup of hot cocoa and a meat sandwich. I watched and listened very closely as the large man talked on the telephone; he was trying to find a warm place for us.

Eventually, we returned to the orphanage, but I never forgot that man's face. I remember how it made me feel deep inside for someone to care about us freezing to death, to care enough to give us blankets and food because we were cold and hungry. It felt good to sit out in that warm hallway and drink cocoa. We sat there for hours, and I was gulping up the attention shown to us by a man whose face had some compassion to it.

I will also never forget the feeling of being hosed down, as though I were an animal. I will never forget those grown up people standing around looking at us kids in a cage. All the while they were laughing, as though we were useless and unworthy of any compassion whatsoever.

The Unspoken Code

"As soon as they turn out the lights, we'll steal some fruit off their trees," said Wayne Evers.

We kids from the orphanage lay quietly in the bushes. We waited what appeared to be hours for the house lights to go off. It was around eleven o'clock in the evening, and there was somewhat of a chill in the air that night. We had run away from the orphanage, and the police had been looking for us for almost three days. We were hungry, we were scared, and we were cold.

Everyone became quiet when a man walked out and shut the garage door. Then the lights inside went out.

"Hey, that looks like the strange man who bought us the hamburgers down at the Krystal yesterday," I whispered to the other boys.

"It sure looked like him," said Wayne.

"It ain't right to steal from someone who's been good to you," said Billy Smith.

"Shut up," said Bill Stroud. "I'm hungry. Let's go and get the damn fruit."

Slowly, through the shadows we made our way across the street, and around the side of his house where the fruit trees were located. We stood there for several minutes looking at one another, waiting to see who would be the first to reach up and steal an orange or a pear from the tree. No one made the first move.

"So he bought us a darn hamburger. Big deal," said Billy.

"Then you pick the fruit first," said Wayne, as he turned around and started walking back toward the street.

I and the other three boys followed Wayne back out into the dark street. As we walked along, we heard Billy running up behind us. As we stopped to wait on him, he ran up holding five or six oranges in his arms.

"Here," he said holding out a large orange.

"I'm hungry, but I don't want any," I told him.

"Me, neither," said one of the other boys.

The four of us turned and started walking toward the old abandoned Spanish house where we always hung out when we ran away.

"Wait. Wait right there," hollered Billy.

He turned around and headed back toward the house with the fruit trees. Several minutes later, he returned without them.

"I put the oranges underneath the tree in a pile," he said.

Wayne reached over and patted Billy on the shoulder.

"I'm hungry," said Wayne. "Let's go and check the garbage cans behind the old church."

Off we went into the night searching for food.

The point of this story is that we, being nine, ten and eleven-year-old kids, had no one to give us any direction in our lives. We knew the difference between right and wrong. However, when you are hungry and your stomach hurts, you will do almost anything to satisfy that hunger. We kids were strictly on our own as far as learning and teaching were concerned. We were like a pack of hungry, wild dogs running up and down the streets of Jacksonville. Many of the kids grew up, and were sent to prison. I do not think that any of us ever hurt or stole anything from anyone who had shown kindness toward us.

For some reason, that seemed to become our code. It was something that we believed in, honored and continued to live by, even after we became adults. I can honestly say that was the only pride and honor that I ever felt as a child. I have often wondered where such a feeling came from.

We kids may have been "evil little bastards," with each of us lacking in love and spirit. However, we as "little criminals" had our own special way of showing certain people that we loved them for being good to us.

"America"

"O beautiful for spacious skies, for amber waves of grain," sang the old man underneath the railroad overpass.

"Can I stand by your fire and get warm?" I asked.

"Sure, kid," he replied, stretching out his arm.

Once again, I had run away from the orphanage—this time for being slapped across the face, because I refused to drink my warm powdered milk.

"Shouldn't you be in school?" asked the old man.

I just stood there warming my hands against the 55-gallon drum. I did not say a word.

"For purple mountain majesties, above the fruited plain," he sang again.

"What's a 'fruited plane'? I asked him, and moved my hand in the air as though it were an airplane.

"Fruited plains, my boy; they are the flat lands of America where all the crops are grown, like corn and wheat."

"I ain't never seen nothing like that before."

"You will one day. America is a very beautiful and wonderful country," he continued.

"How did you get to see all of America?"

"I was in the Navy."

"Was you in the war, too?" I questioned.

"My brothers and I were at Pearl Harbor," he said in a broken voice.

"Do they stay under this bridge with you too?"

"I'm afraid not, son. They were both killed in the Japanese attack."

"America! America! God shed His grace on thee, and crown thy good with brotherhood, from sea to shining sea," he sang. "I love that song!"

I stood there, not having the slightest idea what he was singing or talking about.

"You know, kid. This world is full of two types of people. There are the 'takers' and then there are the 'givers.' Which are you?" he asked raising his eyebrows.

"I don't know."

"Come on boy. Let's go earn something to eat."

He slapped me gently on the back. Then he picked up his backpack and threw it over his shoulder. We began walking down the side of the road.

"You pick up papers, and I'll look for Coca Cola bottles," he instructed.

Hour after hour, we walked beside the road, talking and laughing with each other. By six o'clock that evening, we must have walked ten miles, picking up papers and searching for bottles.

"Bottles are getting a little heavy. Let's cash them in and head back to camp and eat," he stated.

On the way back, we walked into a little roadside store where we traded in the bottles for 56 cents. The old man bought a package of hot dogs, a can of pork 'n' beans, and a can of dog food.

"We ain't going to eat no dog food are we?" I asked.

"You'll see," said the old man.

He was laughing aloud. Just before we got back to the freeway bridge, we stopped in at a gas station. We walked into the washroom, and started to wash our hands and faces.

"Okay, you two deadbeats. Get your butts out of here!" yelled the gas station owner as he pushed the door open with his foot.

The old man said not a word. He just dried his face, and then he walked outside and waited on me.

"And don't come back here."

Then the man spit some chewing tobacco that landed on the shoe of the old man.

"We didn't mean to inconvenience anyone," he told the station owner.

"Just get out of here!"

We took our day's work and headed back to camp. When we arrived, the old man opened the can of beans and the dog food with his knife. Then he raked the dog food out over by the bushes and rinsed the can with the water from his canteen. He cut up the hot dogs into little pieces, mixed them into the beans and divided them between us.

"What's that dog food for?"

"Something will come along that's hungry," he told me.

"You have to eat with the sharp lid kid, so don't cut your tongue."

"Why did we have to pick up all those papers and trash?" I asked him while we ate.

"It's like I told you this morning kid. There are 'takers' in this life, and then there are 'givers.' Most people that I know are 'takers.' Today, we gave a little, and we took a little."

He was smiling from ear to ear.

"America! America! God shed His grace on thee, and crown thy good with brotherhood, from sea to shining sea," he was singing again.

"Are you going to be a 'taker,' or are you going to be a 'giver' when you grown up?" he asked me softly.

"I'm going to be a 'giver.'

"I know you are boy," he said, and smiled at me again.

Later that evening, the police came and took the two of us to the Duval County Jail for loitering. I never saw him again after that. However, I can tell you this: I have never forgotten meeting my first role model.

The Red Ruby Diamond

"Watch it!" yelled out the young man, as he shoved the man backwards, causing him to hit the telephone pole and then fall down into the street.

"You assholes are all over the place," he said.

Then he straightened his coat and tie, and walked away.

"Are you okay?" I asked the man as he began to pick himself up off the ground.

"I'm okay."

"Why did he push you down like that?"

"He thought I was begging for money."

The man began to brush himself off.

"What did you say to him to make him act crazy like that?"

"I asked him if he would step inside the donut shop and get me a few donuts."

"Can't you go in and get some donuts yourself?"

"I'm not allowed on the premises!" he exclaimed loudly.

"What's a premises? I've never heard of that word before?"

"An establishment, or place of business."

"Give me the money, and I'll go in and get the donuts."

The man handed me a dollar, and I went inside to get the order.

"I want twelve donuts in a box," I told the woman behind the counter.

"Are you with him?"

She was pointing to the man standing out on the street.

"I'm just getting him some donuts," I replied.

"Can't sell them to you, kid."

"Why can't I have some donuts?"

"Nothing for him; he is nothing but a vagrant. He's been told to get off this block, and to stop hanging around here bothering our customers."

"But he's hungry. It's unfair not to sell him some food, if he's got money."

"Life ain't fair, kid, and you'll learn that one day. Now, you get out of here too," she said, giving me a dirty look.

I walked back out of the shop, and handed the dollar back to the man. He reached in his pocket, and took out a small money clip. It had a big, red stone in the middle of it. He placed the dollar into the clip, and then stuck it back into his pocket.

"I'm sorry I couldn't get you some donuts to eat," I told him.

"That's okay, kid. I'll eat elsewhere."

He was smiling down at me.

"How come you ain't in school?"

"Can I see that red diamond again?" I asked him, changing the subject.

"Sure," said the man.

He reached into his pocket.

"But it's not a diamond. It's a ruby," he explained. "My wife gave me that clip more than 30 years ago."

"It sure is pretty," I replied as I held it up to the sun.

As we walked along, he talked about his wife. He told me that she had died a few years back, that they had never had any children, and he now lived all alone. As the conversation progressed, I finally told him that I had skipped school, and was from the Children's Home Orphanage, located over on the south side.

"Have you ever been to the zoo?" he asked.

"I went one time, but the matron hit me in the head with a candy apple."

"Let's go to the zoo, kid!"

The next thing I knew, we were in a checkered taxicab and headed to the Jacksonville Zoo. For hours, we walked around looking at all the animals. He did not hurry me along as the matrons did the one time we came to the zoo. We walked, talked, ate ice cream, and he bought me lots of cotton candy. I had never eaten so many bags of peanuts in all my life.

After our visit to the zoo, he took me in a taxicab for a real long drive. When we got to this small town, he took me to visit a great big fort that sat on the edge of the ocean.

"It was a fort from way back in the old time days, when Indians and the Spanish lived here," he told me.

"I never knew that Indians lived in Florida."

He just laughed. As our day ended, the man told me he would drop me off by the orphanage gate when we got back to Jacksonville. He said I should go back, because I could be hurt out in the street. I told him that the matron would beat me because I had skipped school.

"I've had a few switchings in my lifetime," the man told me.

Then he winked at me.

"They don't use any switches on us. They use green bamboo canes, and they hurt real badly, too."

"You'll be okay," said the man, and he patted me on the knee.

When the taxicab stopped in front of Spring Park Elementary School, I got out of the cab and thanked the man for all that he had done for me.

"Kid, you were kind to me this morning and in return, I was kind to you. Being kind to someone costs absolutely nothing. I want you to remember that as you grow up. Can you do that for me?"

"But you spent a lot of money on me. I didn't do nothing for you."

"Oh! Yes, you did, boy. You brought delight and joy into my life for the first time in years."

"Does that make me good for something?"

"You're the best," he said, as he tapped the cab driver on the shoulder.

I stood and watched as the taxi slowly drove away. When I returned to the orphanage, no one said a word to me about missing school. It was as if that day had never even happened at all. That was a wonderful day in my life. I have never forgotten that red ruby diamond, my trip to the zoo, or my visit to the fort. However, most of all,

I will remember being told that I was worth something, and that I brought joy into someone's life. That was a real good feeling.

There is no doubt that my going off with this strange man was a very stupid thing for me to do. My frame of mind at the time, of things unknown to me, had to be much better than the abusive treatment I was receiving at the hands of the orphanage matrons.

Please Don't Tell

"Take off your pants!" ordered the large man.

The two of us just stood there not moving a muscle.

"I said take off your clothing," yelled the man again.

"Why are you going to take our clothes?" I asked.

"Just do as you are told," he demanded, and took several giant steps toward us.

There was many a night that Billy and I slept in the alley behind the Florida Theater. It had been a safe haven to hide in every time the two of us ran away from the orphanage. Many times the police had chased us. However, we had never been assaulted or robbed by anyone who lived out on the streets.

Ten-year-old Billy began to sob as he reached down and began to unbuckle his belt.

"Shut up, you little bastard," screamed the man. He turned around to look down the alley behind him.

"What are you going to do to us?" I asked.

"I'm gonna tear off your balls and stuff them up your little asses," he said, in a slow, drawn out, spooky type of voice.

I just stood there too scared to move, but I reached up and tried to unbutton my shirt.

"YOU, get over by the wall," ordered the man, pointing his finger at Billy.

When I looked sideways, I saw that Billy was completely naked. As he began to move, his legs were shaking so badly that he could hardly walk.

"I ain't got much balls. Really I don't," said Billy.

"You got enough for me."

I stood there holding onto the top button of my shirt. My mind was racing in every direction. I jumped when the large man reached out and grabbed Billy by the arm. He threw him as hard as he could against the brick wall.

"Bend over!"

The man began to unbuckle his own pants. Still crying, Billy leaned against the wall and bent forward. I stood there frozen, as I watched the man grab Billy around the neck and plunge himself against Billy's backside.

"Ow!" screamed Billy. He began to stomp his legs up and down.

My hands began to sling back and forth in every direction, but no matter what I did, I just could not move my body.

"Ow! Ow!" Billy kept screaming.

I looked down and saw an old broken shovel handle that was lying next to the fire we had started earlier. I picked up the shovel and stood there holding it in my hand.

"You move one inch and I'll cut your damn throat," the man said, as he stopped for a moment to look at me. "You got that, you little shit?"

When he turned back to Billy, I took the shovel and scooped up the few embers left from the fire. Quickly I ran toward the man and thrust the hot coals at his backside. The ashes did not reach him, but instead fell into his lowered pants.

"You bastard!" screamed the man. He fell to the ground trying to remove his pants.

I ran over to Billy, grabbed him by the arm, and down the alley we ran. The faster we ran, the more Billy cried. Several blocks down the street, we stopped in the doorway of a large department store.

"We gotta get you some clothes Billy," I told him.

I removed my shirt and wrapped it around him.

"Please don't tell nobody that he did it to me," Billy kept begging, over and over.

"But we gotta tell. You might have a baby now," I said with my eyes open wide.

Within minutes, the police were standing in front of us.

"What is going on here?" asked the police officer.

"I got to tell you something real important!"

"And what might that be?"

I looked over at Billy and saw him lower his head. Several times, I opened my mouth to speak, but no words came out.

"Someone stole my clothes," said Billy in a broken voice.

"Yeah, that's it. Somebody took Billy's clothes, and they ran away," I explained.

Billy and I were taken to the juvenile hall, where we stayed for almost a week. He followed me around day and night afraid I might accidentally tell someone what happened to him. The two of us returned to the orphanage late one Friday evening. Billy never was the same after that. He never smiled, and I never saw him laugh again, not even one time.

The Old Bag Lady

It was not easy for a ten-year-old runaway boy to walk the dangerous streets of Jacksonville, especially at night. Even at that young age, I hated the Children's Home Society where I lived. The orphanage had been my home for almost four years. Little did I know that I still had to live through six more years of hell.

When the school bell rang, I headed out the back door and down Spring Park Road. I traveled for what seemed like miles, before I crossed over the Main Street Bridge. I walked as fast as I could through the downtown area, hunting for something to eat. I made my way down to Bay Street, stopping in the doorway of the Trailways Bus Station. Then I watched as the dirty looking bums drank from their brown paper bags, and argued with each other.

"Sonny, can you go into that store across the street and cash in these here glass bottles for me? I'll buy you a candy," said the old woman.

"Sure. I can do that for you, for nothing."

I loaded the bottles into the store a few at a time. Her large, wooden wagon was loaded with all varieties of soda bottles. I cashed in the bottles, and walked back out of the store to give her the money.

"Can you count the money out for me, sonny?" she asked.

"Can't you count?"

"It's not that, sonny. I just can't see very well."

As I stood there counting out the money in her hand, two large boys walked up and began jerking on her coattail. One boy was trying to grab the money from our hands, while the other boy pulled her backwards. Immediately, I closed my hands and fell to the ground, trying to catch the coins that had fallen.

"Ouch!" I yelled. One boy had stomped on my hand, pinning it to the ground.

"Boy, you sure stink, lady," said one boy.

"You boys go on now. Leave us alone," she yelled at the two of them.

"Shut up you retarded, old bag," yelled the young man. Then he flipped her off as he started across the street with his friend.

I got back down on my knees, and picked up what money had fallen to the ground. Again, I recounted the money and placed it in her hands.

"You sure count awful well, for being little like you are. And you can count fast, too," she said as she laughed.

"Are you retarded, too, like me?" I asked her.

"You ain't retarded boy. You are as smart as a whip. Look how fast you can count. And you are real cute, too."

"You really think so?" I asked with a big smile on my face.

For the remainder of the day, I walked around talking with the old woman. I stayed as close to her as possible, hoping she would again say something nice about me. Throughout the years, I have often thought about that woman, especially when I drive through a large city and see someone pushing a shopping cart down the street. I could count on one hand the times that any grown adult ever gave me a compliment, or made me feel proud of myself. The few times that it did happen, I soaked up the experience like a sponge soaking up water.

I can remember exactly what she looked like, and exactly how she smelled. I remember her legs being fat at the ankles with many veins. Her lips were rough and cracked, her hands scarred, and she had many sores about her hands and wrists. However, what I remember most was her kind face. She had a wonderful smile that made her look happy all the time.

Late that afternoon, we parted company. She told me she wanted to have a drink or two at the bar on the corner, and no children were allowed. As she drank, I stood outside the bar room door watching her as she laughed and talked. After about fifteen minutes, I headed on down the road to who-knows-where.

I never saw her again after that. However, that was okay with me. She gave me what I needed that day—the thought that I was very cute, I was not dumb, and best of all, that I was "as smart as a whip." Her kind words followed me for many years. However, what I learned most from her was that being kind to others costs a person absolutely nothing, except maybe a few moments of her time.

For No Reason At All

The two of us had not eaten for almost three days. Generally, the restaurants would dump their scraps into the dumpster located in the alleyway at the end of each shift. However, for some unknown reason, there was no food to be found. We had been on the run for two days. We left the orphanage at about seven o'clock Friday evening. We planned to head for California as soon as we raised enough money to start hitchhiking.

Wayne Evers had just turned eleven the week before, and I was a few months younger than he was. We were used to the streets of Jacksonville. We had run away many times, and we never had a problem finding food or raising money. For hours, we wandered from restaurant to restaurant looking in the garage cans in search of food.

As we passed a large, red brick church on Park Street, we noticed a man standing behind a restaurant peeling potatoes. We watched as he peeled each one and then threw it into a large metal tub. We must have stood there for five minutes just watching, neither one of us saying a word. We automatically knew that dinner was nearby. Once the man finished peeling, he reached down, grabbed the water hose and began washing the potatoes. With eyes opened wide, we watched as he cleaned up the peelings, and packed them into a large paper bag. As he was about to throw the skins into the garage can, he looked up and saw us staring at him.

"Can I help you boys?" he yelled out.

"We're just looking," Wayne yelled back at him.

"You two boys might as well head on down the road. You are not getting these here potatoes," he said, in a somewhat gruff sounding voice.

"We were going to ask if we could have those peeling skins," said Wayne.

"You ain't getting them either," he said, as he opened the door and sat the bag inside.

"Ain't you just going to throw them away anyway? Ain't that what you were going to do?" I asked.

"You two get out of here, before I call the police. You hear me?"

"But we are hungry. Can we please have the peelings?" I begged.

The man stood there for several moments, and then said, "I'll tell you what. You boys clean up all these papers, hose down this back area, and I'll give you the peelings."

"That's a deal!" hollered Wayne.

We began running around the small lot picking up the papers and trash. Within thirty minutes, the area was very clean. I turned on the water, and began to hose down the cement for as far as the small hose would reach. When we were done, we walked up to the back door, and began to knock. After three or four knocks, the door jerked open, and there stood the man with a very angry look on his face.

"I thought I told you little tramps to get the hell out of here," he screamed.

"But you said…," I started to say.

"The police are on their way. You had best get your little asses on the move," he said, as he came walking toward us.

Wayne and I backed up as the large man neared where we were standing. We did not stop until we reached the sidewalk.

"That's not a fair thing to do," said Wayne.

"And we're hungry," I blurted out.

"I don't give a rat's ass, if you little bastards starve to death," said the man, as he looked down the street to see if the police were coming.

"But we weren't asking for something for free. It was something that you were going to throw away. And besides, we worked for it," I hollered.

"You two are a couple of stupid fools."

"But don't you care if we are hungry?" Wayne asked.

I reached over and slapped Wayne on the arm when I saw a police car pull up to the red light and stop. He and I took off running between the large buildings. We did not stop until we were at least ten blocks away from the restaurant.

It is strange how that incident affected my life. Each time I peel potatoes, I think about that fellow, and how hungry two boys were at the time. However, more than that, I will always remember how cruel people can be to one another, for no reason whatsoever. I have always understood being mistreated in the orphanage, but why would anyone in the outside world be cruel to another human being for absolutely no reason? To this day, that is something I have never been able to understand.

No Feelings

"The record before me indicates that you are constantly getting into trouble. What seems to be the problem?" asked the judge.

"I don't know why I get into trouble all the time. I do not mean to do bad things. I really don't, sir."

"It appears to me to be a matter of just doing what one is told. Now that doesn't seem very hard to do."

Once again, I was standing before Judge Marion Gooding of the Duval County Juvenile Court in Jacksonville. I had just turned ten years old, and for some reason, I was once again standing before a juvenile judge who knew me well.

"What is it that you feel when you get into trouble?" asked the judge.

"I don't know."

"It appears to me that you don't know anything. It's the same story each and every time that you come before me," he said, pointing his pencil at me.

I just stood there biting my bottom lip. I did not have the slightest idea of what to say to him.

"What is it you feel right now," he asked.

"I don't feel nothing."

"Nothing at all?"

"No, sir," I responded, shaking my head back and forth.

"Are you scared right now?" the judge inquired.

"I'm a little bit scared."

"Then you do feel something, right?"

"Yes, sir. I guess."

"It says here that you are constantly climbing trees, and that you are digging holes in the ground. Do you know that is very dangerous, and somewhat destructive of property"?

"It don't hurt no trees to climb on them."

"And what about the holes you dig in the ground?" he questioned.

"We just build army forts, and we cover them up with wood and dirt. Then we play army war."

"That is not really the question. The question here is why you cannot do what you are told?"

I just stood there with my head down. For the life of me, I could not understand why I was standing before Judge Gooding. This was my third or fourth time before the judge. Each time was because I had done something simple, like climbing on the chain-link fence at the orphanage or refusing to eat eggplant or slimy okra.

"What we have here, Your Honor, is a criminal in the making. He is very destructive, and very unruly. He just will not listen to direction," said Mrs. Winters, the head matron of the orphanage.

I looked up to see the judge looking directly at me. All he did the entire time she was speaking was sit there, constantly tapping his pencil on the top of his large desk.

"Has the boy ever been tested for mental retardation?" asked the Judge.

No one answered. The courtroom fell silent for more than a minute, while the judge wrote something down on his pad. I had heard those words before, and I knew what they meant. It meant that you were not right inside your head.

"I got to stop doing bad things, or everyone's going to think that I got retardation inside my head," I thought to myself.

"Let's put the boy upstairs for ten days. I'll order some tests, and I'll make a decision based on those results," ordered the judge.

A few minutes later, I was taken upstairs. Several men in black suits locked me in a wire cage. The next day, I was given several tests with many questions on them. They were very easy kinds of questions too. I did not have any problem answering all of them, because I lied on most of them. Four days later, I was back in court.

"Mrs. Winters, the tests that were given to Roger Dean Kiser do indicate that the boy has some severe emotional problems," said the judge.

"I think it goes much deeper than that, Your Honor!" said Mrs. Winters.

I stood there wondering how they had reached such a conclusion. I knew, without a doubt, that I had answered all the questions correctly.

"Do you think that you can behave if I send you back to the children's home?" the judge asked.

"But there's nothing to do, if we can't climb tress and build forts in the ground."

"What do you have for the children as far as recreation?" the judge asked Mrs. Winters.

"There is a swing set, and we have a large library in the boys dormitory."

"We have one roller skate," I told the judge.

The judge placed his finger over his mouth, as if to tell me to keep quiet.

"How do you feel now? What are your feelings?" he inquired as he placed his chin on both his hands.

"I still don't got no feelings no more," I told him, as I shook my head back and forth.

Over the next four years, I stood before the judge twenty or thirty more times. My crimes ranged from climbing in the orphanage trees to stealing from a local Mexican restaurant. Then I graduated on to smoking grape vines. By the time I was fourteen, I had a juvenile record that was six inches thick. The final straw came when several of us appeared in court before Judge Gooding. This time we were charged with killing animals.

I knew that it was hopeless, so I said not a word. Mrs. Winters stood before the court telling her lies. She told the court that I had taken all the fish out of the aquarium at school, and flushed them down the toilet. She knew that one of the other boys had dumped ink into the aquarium, and that I had taken the fish out of the ink stained water, so that they would not die. She knew that I had placed them in the toilet, so that they would not die from the ink. She had flushed the fish down the toilet.

I stood there watching her as she did it. As the goldfish washed around and around in the bowl, she looked me straight in the eye and said, "Now you are out of here for good, you little bastard!"

You Are Already Dead

I held my breath as he pushed the revolver deep into the side of my neck.

"We were not going to steal from you. Honest, we were not. We only steal food from the stores. That's all!"

Those were the broken words that I tried to force from my constricted throat. I had met a ten-year-old boy, same age as me, in the city park several hours earlier. We had stolen several packs of cigarettes from the local gas station, and were running because the owner was chasing us. It was dark, so we ducked into an alley to hide. We watched as the gas station owner ran right past us. The next thing I knew, a strange man had a gun pushed into the side of my neck. Slowly, the man eased the gun away from my neck, allowing me to breathe.

"You're a lying little bastard," he said.

He gritted his teeth, and moved the barrel of the gun within an inch of my right eye. I stood perfectly still, looking at the hole in the end of the weapon.

"We weren't doing anything. We just came in here so the police won't find us," said my friend.

"Shut up!" yelled the man.

I had no idea what he was going to do. I could smell liquor on his breath, and I wondered if I should try to reason with him. All at once, my new friend began running down the alley. I could hardly believe it when the man pointed the gun in his direction and fired twice. The boy hit the ground, and lay there motionless.

"You're next you little shit!" he screamed.

I broke loose from his grip, and backed up against the brick wall. I could hardly believe it when the boy suddenly jumped up and began running again. The man began to chase him, waving his gun and yelling. I looked behind me and saw that there was no way to escape, as the alley came to a dead end. I started walking toward the entrance of the alley. I had taken less than five steps when the stranger appeared again. He just stood there, looking at me. I was sweating more than I had ever sweated in my entire life.

"That little shit got away, but you won't."

He started walking toward me.

"Are you really going to kill me?" I asked him, in a broken voice.

"You're one dead little fucker."

"I don't care. I don't care a damn," I said, even though I was standing there trembling like a trapped mouse.

"Don't hand me that sob story line of bullshit!"

"Really, I really don't care."

"You two were going to rob me, weren't you?" he growled.

"No, sir! We were stealing cigarettes from that gas station with the red horse on the sign, and the man that was chasing us."

"Let me see the cigarettes," he said, slipping the gun into his waistband.

I reached in my pants pocket, took out two crushed packs of cigarettes, and handed them to the man. He examined both packs very carefully.

"You got any matches?" he asked.

I reached into my back pocket, and took out ten packs of matches that we had also stolen.

The man stuck one pack of cigarettes in his shirt pocket, and began hitting the other pack against the back of his hand. He opened the pack, took out a cigarette with his teeth, and handed it to me. He struck a match, and gave us both a light.

"How come you are not scared?" he questioned.

"I don't know. I just ain't. But ain't you worried about the cops coming in this here alley after hearing you shoot that gun off?" I asked him.

"Now that you mentioned it, I suppose I should get my ass on down the road."

"You still going to kill me?"

"Why should I kill you kid? You told me you did not give a damn if I killed you. If that really is the case, then you are just like me. You are already dead."

I watched him as he picked up several personal items, and headed down the alleyway.

"Can I have some of those there cigarettes?" I hollered.

He never said a word. He just kept on walking.

The I.O.U.

"It's been two days now, and all we've had is a couple of candy bars. We need to get some real food inside us," said Johnny Nash.

It was late on Sunday evening, and it was very cold. Three of us boys, all ranging in ages from ten to eleven, had once again run away from the orphanage. We made our planned escape shortly after the Spring Park Elementary School bell rang on Friday afternoon. When leaving, we had a total of 75 cents between us. We each had saved our "milk money" for five days. We hoped that 75 cents would be enough money to feed ourselves, until we could find jobs and get a place of our own.

The orphanage was nothing short of a living hell. The beatings, the abuse, and the molestations took place almost on a daily basis. I am not exactly sure if that is actually why we ran away. Myself, I ran away because I felt I was entitled to. It made me feel safe when I ran away. Though I was not very smart doing school things, there was something inside my head that told me what was happening to me was wrong. I was smart enough to know that somewhere, someday, someone would come along and help me.

We boys made our way along Park Street, weaving our way in and out of buildings and trying to stay one step ahead of the police. The officers knew us well, and we knew they would be looking for us. As we rounded one of the buildings, someone yelled out at us.

"Hey, kids. Come here," said a young man who was standing by an old black car.

"Yes, sir," I replied.

"Do you boys know where to get some gasoline?"

"At the gas station," said Johnny.

"I know that," said the man. "I mean some gas to siphon."

"You mean steal some gas with a hose and a can?" I asked him.

The man turned to Johnny, and held out a package of graham cracker cookies.

"It's almost dark. You fellows get some gas, and you can have these here snack crackers," he told us.

We agreed that after dark, we would try to find a car from which we could siphon gas. The man gave us a five-gallon can and a long piece of black rubber hose. He got back into his car, and the three of us hid in the bushes behind one of the buildings. When it was dark, we made our way down one of the side streets, hunting for gas.

"Look! There is a truck with 'Shell' on the side of it. That has to have gas in it. It's from a gas station," whispered Donald.

Slowly, in the darkness, we made our way up to the truck. Very carefully, I opened the gas tank lid, and stuck the hose into the vehicle. When it hit the bottom of the tank, I began to suck on the end of the hose until the gas started running out. I placed the end of the hose into the gas can, and I waited.

"What you doing, boy?" yelled someone.

Then he grabbed me by the back of my neck, and raised me off the ground. When I looked up, I saw the biggest black man that I had ever seen in my entire lifetime. He looked bigger and meaner than a giant I had seen in that *Jack and the Bean Stalk* book at the orphanage. I just shook with fear. Johnny and Donald took off running back toward Park Street.

"Boy! Do you like taking what don't belong to you?" he asked, as he sat my feet back down on the ground.

"We were just trying to get some food," I told him.

My eyes were open as big as saucers.

"Looks to me like you're trying to steal my gas," he said pointing down at the gas can.

I explained to him that we were hungry, and we were trading the gas for crackers, so we could eat. He took the gas can and the hose, and he sat them in the back of his truck.

"Give me your shoes, and get in the truck," he ordered as he unlocked the door.

"Yes, sir," I said.

I immediately hopped up into the truck. My heart was beating 90 miles per hour as I took off my shoes and handed them to him.

"Where them other two boys at?" he asked.

"I don't know."

"Looks like them right there."

He pulled over to the side of the roadway.

"Tell them to come over here," he demanded.

"Donald! Johnny! You got to come here," I yelled out the truck window.

Slowly, they made their way over to the truck.

"Why you boys want to take what don't belong to you?" the man asked.

"'Cause we was hungry," said Johnny.

"Get in the back of the truck."

"I'm gonna kick your ass," said Johnny as he pointed his finger at me.

The two boys climbed into the back of the truck, and off we drove.

"Are you going to turn us in to the cops?" I asked the man.

"I should. But I ain't."

Several minutes later, he pulled into a small restaurant, and parked.

"Let's go inside and get a bite to eat," he said, as he got out of the truck.

We all walked into the restaurant, where the man bought us each a sandwich and an order of French fries. After we had eaten, he went out to his truck and came back in with a clipboard. He tore off a piece of paper, and wrote something down on it.

"I want each of you boys to sign this here paper."

He pushed the paper across the table.

"What is it?" I asked.

"It's called an I.O.U.," he said.

"What does I.O.U. mean?" asked Johnny.

"It means that you owe me for this here meal. And if you don't pay me, you will go to jail," he advised us.

The three of us signed the paper. The man folded it up and stuck it in his shirt pocket. Then he got up from the table.

"You boys finish your meal, and then you head back to wherever. Understand?" he said, looking over the top of his glasses.

"Thank you for the food," I told him.

He winked.

"You come out to the truck with me and get your shoes," he told me.

He and I walked out to the truck, where he handed me my shoes.

"I'll pay you for the meal one day. I really will. I am going to be famous. Just like Al Capone, except I ain't never going to hurt nobody," I told him.

"Why would you want to be like Al Capone?"

"'Cause he's got lots of money and clothes. I bet he's got lots of food, too!"

"Maybe you could be a movie star and become famous?" he said

"I can never be a movie star, 'cause the orphanage says that I got big ears that make me look ugly.

The man reached into his pocket and took out the paper that we had signed. He pushed the small note down into my shirt pocket.

"Don't say anything to the other boys. Make them sweat it for a while," he said, as he got up into his truck.

I was in Jacksonville, Florida day before yesterday. I drove over to Park Street to have a look around. That restaurant was no longer there, and the lot was vacant, except for the tall weeds. The old machine shop, which had belonged to my old friend Mr. Lewis, was now vacant, as were the rest of the old brick buildings in the neighborhood. There was now a paint store located on the corner where Donald Watts and his mother had lived in an old shack.

It is strange how we humans tend to think and feel. I suppose I now buy Shell gasoline, because of a feeling placed inside of me by a strange black man more than 45 years ago. I suppose I have never been prejudiced, because a stranger that was black took the time to be kind to me and my friends.

Different Lifestyles

It would be impossible to count the times that we boys ran away from the Children's Home Orphanage. Sometimes it was just for fun. Other times, it was to find food, or just to get away from being beaten. Once again, we had come to one of our favorite hiding places. It was a city park located across the St. John's River on Park Street, near Five Points.

It was late November, and the evenings were quite chilly. The sun was starting to set behind the large oak trees that surrounded the park. We boys always stuck together because of the local gangs who frequented the park during the evening hours. Generally, the gangs would not bother us. They knew we were only ten or eleven years old, and we did not have any money or possessions.

As darkness fell, the gangs would walk the perimeter of the park waiting for the "queers" to come out. There was not a night that one or two of these gay men were not severely beaten. It was very hard for us to understand. Why would they constantly come back to the park almost every evening, knowing what might happen to them? Many times the police would find them—some almost unconscious—and they would be arrested and hauled off to jail. However, there were times when the men were beaten so badly that they could not get up off the ground. Many times we would hide in the bushes and watch as the police took out their leather slapjack. Then they removed the men's shoes, and beat the bottoms of their feet until they were bloody.

I will forever remember lying in the bushes, night after night, watching police officers beat on people as if they were animals. I remember well the high-pitched screams as the men were beaten. I remember them begging and pleading for the police to stop. I still see a picture in my mind of a man's body as it twisted back and forth like a snake trying to get away. We later learned this was the cops' way of making sure many of these men would not come back to the park for a week or two. It was also their way of exposing to the public that this individual was a secret homosexual.

I will never forget the laughing of the police officers, as they appeared to enjoy what they were doing. I remember feeling helpless and scared. I remember thinking that the world outside the orphanage was a terrible place to be. For as long as I live, I will forever remember there are human beings on this earth who will always use their power to hurt others.

There was one night when I was sure the police had almost killed one man. When they left, we came out from the bushes and tried to help him. He could not remember who he was, or where he lived. His feet were so sore that he could not walk. I remember looking him up and down, and wondering why the police thought he was different from the rest of us. When I talked to him, he appeared to be very kind, but he had a very soft, high-pitched voice. He seemed to be concerned why we were out at such a late and unsafe hour. We sat talking with him until he got himself together. I never spoke to him the entire time. I just sat there on the ground and watched as passing car lights hit his face. None of us was used to being around people who were kind.

As bad as these experiences were, they have had a very positive effect on my life. Those terrible things have caused me, for some reason, to always root for the underdog. They have taught me not to be judgmental of others. I have learned to treat others as they treat me. I have learned that I may not agree with the way others think, or how they believe, but I have the right to disagree with someone's lifestyle. Even as a young confused little boy, I knew that it costs nothing to be kind, and that it was wrong to hurt someone.

My friendship has always been available to anyone who wanted to be kind to me. All that I ask in return for that friendship is that they treat me with respect, and not hurt me.

The Champon

"Hey! Look at this. I think it's made out of real honest to goodness gold," said Tommy Jernigan, as he held up the trophy he had discovered in the large garbage dumpster.

"That can't be real gold. Nobody's going to throw away something made out of real gold," said one of the other boys who lived in the orphanage with us.

As boys of ten and eleven years of age, we had decided to run away from the Children's Home Orphanage to venture out into a new world to find safety. The five of us closely gathered around Tommy, so that we could see what was inscribed on the trophy.

"You are truly a champon," read the plaque attached to the wooden part of the base.

"What's a champon?" asked one of the boys.

"It's a horse. I seen it on TV," another boy replied.

"Why would someone give a horse a trophy?" asked Robert.

No one said a word. We just stood there looking at the beautiful shiny trophy.

"Can I help you boys?" said someone walking up from behind us.

We turned to see a large man walking towards us.

"What you got there?" asked the man.

Tommy tried to hide the trophy behind him.

"It's a champon trophy," said Tommy, pulling the trophy from behind him and holding it toward the stranger.

"Is this made out of real gold?" asked Tommy.

"I don't think so," said the man, smiling as he spoke.

"Let me see what you have there," he told Tommy.

The man took the trophy from Tommy's hands, and he stood there carefully looking at it.

"Well boys. The word 'champion' has been misspelled. That's evidently why someone threw the trophy away."

"Is champon a horse on TV?" asked Emmett.

"I don't know about that. This kind of 'champion' means that you are good at doing something very special. Things like baseball or swimming.

"Is it okay if we have it?" asked Tommy.

"I don't see why not," said the man, as he handed the trophy back to Tommy.

We took the golden prize back to the orphanage where we kept it in our underground fort. There were days when we would light a small fire made from leaves, just so that we could see the trophy glimmer its golden color. Once a week, we would have a foot race to determine which one of us boys would get to sit with the trophy. It would sit in front of the winner of the race when we held our meetings inside the fort.

In more than ten years in the orphanage, I cannot recall one time when any of us kids were told we were special or that we were loved. However, I do remember winning that gold trophy many times, as do the other boys who were there with me. We boys will forever remember the pride that came from that little golden trophy. It was just a worthless piece of metal and wood found in an old garbage dumpster—a worthless trophy that gave us kids a little bit of a head start in life by letting us know the feeling that we, too, could one day grow up to be "champons."

You Can Tell By The Eyes

"You're just like Mother Winters at the orphanage," I told the man, as he began to choke me.

"Just give me those hot dogs, and I'll turn you loose," he said.

I opened my hand and let the package of hot dogs fall to the ground. The man released me, grabbed the frozen package, and began to rip it open with his teeth. I stood watching as he tried to bite into the frozen meat.

"It's still like frozen. I just stole it a little while ago," I advised him.

The man paid me no mind. All his attention was focused on getting the food into his stomach. As I turned and began to walk away, I heard him say, "Who is this Mother Winters. Is that your mother?"

I stopped dead in my tracks. I did not even turn around.

"No, I don't got no real mother."

"Then who is Mother Winters?"

"She's the matron at the orphanage where I live over on the south side."

"Ain't no orphanages around no more," he blurted out, pushing his bushy eyebrows upward, almost to his hairline.

"There's one where I live."

"Come here, boy," he said.

He held out several hot dogs. Very carefully, I walked back over to where he was standing. I reached out and took two franks from his hand.

"You know, I might have killed you had you not given me this here food."

"I ain't never gonna kill nobody 'cause of food," I replied.

"You will, if you get hungry enough."

He gave me a very stern, hard look. I just stood there shaking my head back and forth. As I began to eat, the man watched my every bite. The faster I would eat, the faster the man would stuff the food in his mouth. It became apparent to me that he did not want to share any additional food.

"How old are you boy?"

"Eleven," I answered.

"Let me tell you something. When you get food, you had best keep it hid, and hid very well. Find yourself a hole and climb in deep. Eat all you can and then get gone."

I stood there staring at him for the longest time. My eyes never left his face. I wanted to see if I thought that he would really kill somebody. His movements were slow and jerky. He reminded me of a cat that I had seen run over by an old, black car just a week before. His butt was all mashed on the road, but he was still alive. I tried to help him, but he was really mean, and I could tell by his eyes that he wanted to kill me. I saw that same look in this man's eyes. I chewed, swallowed the last of the cold hot dog, and began to walk away.

"See you tomorrow, kid," yelled the man, as he laughed aloud.

I kept walking, and never looked back. I was just too scared.

Right and Wrong

I cannot count the times I ran away from the Children's Home Orphanage. I know it had to be in the hundreds. I was eleven years old in 1957. I remember feeling very alone as I walked along Park Avenue. I was hungry, I was cold and I had nowhere to go.

"Hey, boy," yelled a heavy-set man standing in the doorway of a machine shop.

"Yes, sir," I said.

"You want to make a couple of dollars?"

"Yes, sir!"

"I would like for you to go down to the liquor store at the end of the block, and get me a pint of whiskey. Can you do that for me?" he asked.

"I can do that for two dollars."

He walked back into the shop, took a $20 bill out of the cash register, and handed it to me. I stood there looking at the large bill, as I had never held that much money before. That was all the money in the world, as far as I was concerned. I turned and started walking down the block to find the liquor store. As I looked back, I saw the man disappear out of the doorway. When I turned the corner, I started to run as fast as I could. In those few moments, I had decided to keep the $20 to feed myself. I did not intend on bringing it back to him. Within a few minutes, I was blocks away. I sat down on the city bus bench gasping for air. Sitting there, I looked at both sides of the $20.

"This will feed me for a long, long time. Maybe even buy me a place to live," I thought to myself.

All of a sudden, a very strange feeling started to come over me. Even to this day, I am not sure what that feeling was. All I knew for sure was that what I was doing would be hurting that man. I sat there for several minutes trying to make that feeling go away, but it would not. I got up off the bench, and started running back toward the small shop. When I reached the liquor store, I went inside and purchased a pint of whiskey. I put all the money into the paper sack with the bottle, and returned to the machine shop.

"I was wondering why it took you so long," said the man, as I walked in.

He took the money and the small bottle out of the brown paper sack, and handed me $2. Looking down at the ground, I thanked him. He patted me on the shoulder, and I walked out of his shop. As I walked along Park Avenue, that same feeling came over me once again. It just would not go away. I turned around and walked back to the machine shop. Walking up to the man, I held out the $2 he had given me.

"I was going to take your whole $20, and was not going to come back," I told him.

"But you did come back. That is what is important."

"But I still have that bad feeling," I replied.

The man reached out, took the $2 from my hand, and stuck it in his front pocket.

"I'm going to show you how to get rid of that feeling."

All day long, I worked cleaning up his shop. Many times I cut myself, and my hands bled from the metal shavings I picked up off the floor. By the end of the day, I had numerous bandages from the tips of my fingers to my elbows. I watched him make hundreds of metal parts; pieces used in the space program for rockets. At seven o'clock that evening, he called me into his little office.

"Let's see now. You have worked ten hours. I will pay you $2.12 an hour for ten hours work. That comes to $21.20."

I held out my hand as he counted out the money.

"Am I still a stealer?" I asked.

"No! You are not a stealer, boy. Not by a long shot."

After leaving the machine shop, I stopped every block or so to see if that bad feeling would come back, but it never did!

Over the next fifteen years, I would return now and then to have lunch with Mr. Lewis in his little run down machine shop. I am so thankful that I met someone along the way—someone who took the time to teach me there was a right way and a wrong way to make $20.

Shoes and Hugs

It is amazing that any of us boys from the orphanage ever passed from grade to grade. Once again, five of us had not gone to school. Running away again, we headed out into a world that was unknown to us. Generally, we would cross the Main Street Bridge, and walk the ten miles over to Park Street. We would hang around in the small city park located next to the Five Points shopping area.

"Look at that old man on the bench. He ain't got no shoes on, just socks," said Wayne Evers.

We stood looking at the dirty, unshaven man. He appeared to be resting. We walked closer to the bench where he sat, and stood there looking at him.

"It's cold, mister. How come you ain't got no shoes?"

He opened his eyes and looked at each one of us, then closed his eyes again without saying a word.

"It's cold, mister. How come you ain't got any shoes?" Wayne asked again.

"They just fell apart several days ago," mumbled the old man, nodding his head to one side.

"Ain't you got no more money to get more shoes?"

"You boys had best just move on," said the man.

Then he lay back down on the bench.

"Why don't you go home and sleep?" asked Billy.

The old man turned over on the bench, and said not a word.

We started walking down the sidewalk, headed toward the large fishpond. There we would hide behind the large bushes, so the police could not see us. Every hour or so, we would venture out of the park to check out the garbage cans behind several of the local restaurants. Other than stealing, eating from these cans was the only way we could get food. At three o'clock in the afternoon, after school let out, we felt we could safely venture around the Five Points Plaza without being hassled by the police. As we walked around looking in the store windows, we came upon a shoe store.

"God! Look at all them hundreds of shoes," yelled Billy Stroud. "Here they got all those shoes, and that old man ain't got any."

"Want to steal him some shoes?" asked Wayne.

No one said a word; we just stood there looking at each other.

"Who's going to run in and get 'em?" I asked.

"I'll get them," said Wayne.

"But we ain't got no right size," said Billy.

"All you got to get is a big size. Get real big," I instructed Wayne.

Within a split second, Wayne had run into the shoe store and grabbed a box of shoes off the rack. Then out the door he went in a flash. We watched him as he ran full blast down Park Street toward the park. We just stood there, unable to move. We could not believe that he had stolen a pair of shoes that fast, and we also could not believe that no one was chasing him. No one even came out of the store. The four of us stood there for several more minutes. Still, nothing happened. We finally started walking back toward the park. As we crossed the street, we saw Wayne standing by the bench with the old man. As we approached them, we noticed the old man was trying on the shoes.

"They are a little big on me, but I can wear more socks," the old man told him.

"Did you boys steal these here shoes?" asked the man.

"No, sir. We collected Coca Cola bottles all day," Wayne lied.

The old man smiled and looked over at Wayne.

"Come here boy."

Wayne walked over to the man, and stopped in front of him. The dirty old man stood up and wrapped his arms around Wayne.

"Thank you much, boy."

At that very moment, everything got quiet. Wayne just stood there with his body totally limp. He had no idea what to do with his arms. When the man freed Wayne from his grip, Wayne turned his back toward us. He walked over and stopped by a tree near the pond. All at once, he slapped the tree as hard as he could. No one said a word. Several minutes later, the five of us walked over to Riverside Avenue, heading back toward the Main Street Bridge that headed back to the orphanage. Still, no one said a word, not for ten blocks or so.

Suddenly someone yelled out, "Wayne got a huggggg. Wayne got a huggggg."

All at once, there was total chaos on the street. Everyone began to push and shove each other as if it were a bar room brawl. Fifteen seconds later, all was once again quiet. I looked up at Wayne, and I saw tears in his eyes. I winked at Wayne, and smiled. He walked over and put his arm around my shoulder. I, in turn, put my arm around the shoulder of Billy Stroud, and he around another boy, and he around another.

That is just the way life was with us orphans on the streets.

All Dressed Up and Nowhere To Go

"Excuse me. Do you have any work that I could do to earn 50 cents?" I asked the large man standing in the doorway of the small shop.

"Why do you need 50 cents?" he said.

"I want to buy some Krystal burgers to eat."

"Why aren't you in school this time of day," he asked me, scratching his head.

I just stood there, and did not say a word.

"I've seen you around here several times before. You are one of those runaway kids from the orphanage over on the south side of town, ain't you?"

"I just don't like it there any more," I told him.

"Don't they feed you at the orphanage?"

"Just bunches of slimy okra with a lot of hair on it, lots and lots of eggplant, and a whole bunch of bread with peanut butter and jelly all mixed together," I told him.

"Don't they ever feed you children any meat?"

"Yeah, we got meat, but it's got green like things in it sometimes. It tastes very bad like, too. I don't like to eat it."

"How long you been a runaway now?"

"Almost a week," I replied.

Where have you been staying?" he asked as he leaned up against the red brick building.

"Over on Riverside Avenue, in those old brick buildings by the St. John's River."

The man reached into his pocket, and he took out a pack of cigarettes.

"Can I have one of those?" I asked.

He reached out and handed me one of the cigarettes.

"How old are you, boy?"

"Eleven," I told him. "Have you ever gone fishing for real fish?"

I watched as he struck a match and lit his cigarette. Then he bent over, and he lit mine.

"How long you been smoking cigarettes?"

"Ever since I was nine, almost two years now."

"You ever been fishing for real fish?" I asked him again.

"Used to fish a lot when I was a kid. My daddy took me fishing all the time. I have been too busy the last few years to do any fishing."

He stood there blowing smoke rings from his mouth.

"How can you do that?" I asked, watching the rings come from his mouth one after the other.

"So you like to fish?"

"Never been real fishing, except in a goldfish pond near the orphanage. I got in bad trouble, too. I got a bad beating with a bamboo stick," I told him.

"Well, I have to close up now. You ever ate pork chops?" he asked.

"What's a pork chops?"

"Let me lock up, and I'll feed you a meal you'll never forget," he said, laughing aloud.

I followed him around as he locked up his small shop. Then he grabbed a pile of old newspapers off his desk. We walked around the building,, and I opened the passenger door to the old pickup truck. I slid in beside him and folded my hands on my lap. As we drove along, he began to sing to himself. Within five minutes, we pulled up in front of a house that was near the hospital off Riverside Avenue. There was a large woman sitting on the front porch.

"You wait in the truck until I motion for you to come up."

I nodded my head back and forth to let him know that I understood. He talked with the woman on the porch, and she looked over at me several times. Then he waved for me to come up on the porch.

"This is my wife, Judy, and this is... hell, I don't even know your name," said the large man. "What's your name, boy?"

"Roger Dean Kiser. That is Roger Dean Kiser, with an RDK. That's my initials," I told them.

They both laughed, and then they sat down on the porch swing. I sat down on the cement step, and I watched as they talked with each other. They let me stay at their home Friday, Saturday and Sunday. All three nights, I got to take a bath in a real bathtub. They even had yellow soap in a bottle to wash your hair. I slept in a great big bed all by myself, and we ate food that I had never seen before. On Saturday morning, the man took me fishing on his little boat, and I caught a real fish for the very first time. When we got back to his house, his wife took me to the store, and bought me a new set of clothes, and a new pair of cowboy boots. We looked all over for a cowboy hat, but we could not find one. When we got back to the house, the man gave me his old fishing hat to wear.

On Sunday, we got up early, and we all went to church. I did not mind church at all. It was fun, even though my butt hurt from the hard wooden seat. When church was over, we ate a great big chicken with corn bread and thick gravy. After lunch, the man told me that he wanted to talk with me out on the front porch.

"You can't tell anyone that you were here, or I will get into serious trouble. Tomorrow I will take you back to my shop and you need to go back to the children's home. You need to stay there, and you need to go to school. That is very important. Do you understand?" he asked, sternly.

"Why can't I stay here and live with you?" I asked him.

"It's against the law."

"But you ain't got nobody, and I ain't got anybody."

"Look here, son. My wife is very sick, and I have to work all the time. There is no way that we can have children living here."

All the wonderful feelings that I had for three days seemed to disappear in an instant. I just sat there with my head held down, eyes looking at the ground.

"Would you like to go to the movies?" he asked.

"No, sir," I said quietly.

We spoke very little for the remainder of the evening. We had chicken sandwiches for supper, with iced tea that had sugar cubes inside. The next morning when I got up, I put on my new clothes and boots, and then we ate breakfast. Without speaking, we started the drive back to his small shop. All at once, he pulled off to the side of the road.

"Before I drop you off, is there anything that you would like?" he asked.

"Anything?"

"What would you like?" he asked again.

"Can I have my very own pack of cigarettes?"

He pulled back onto the road, drove about a block, and then pulled into a gas station, and got out of the truck.

"What kind of cigarettes do you smoke?"

"The White Parliaments with the recessed filters," I said.

I watched him as he purchased several packs of cigarettes. When he came back to the truck, he pitched them at me through his window. Not a word was said as he and I drove back to his shop. When we arrived, we got out of the truck, and walked to the front of the building. He kept looking down into my eyes, as he searched out his keys.

"I hope you enjoyed your stay with us. You head on back to the orphan home, and do not run away anymore. It is dangerous. You hear me?" he said.

"Thank you for the new pants and the new shirt. I really like them a lot," I told him.

"My pleasure, boy. Now you go on back to the orphan home now."

I turned and started walking toward Riverside Avenue to see if I could find Robert and Wayne, the two boys who had run away with me. When I got to the old brick building where we usually stayed, they were not there. I began walking toward the city, and when I reached the downtown area, I stopped in front of one of the shops. For the longest time, I just stood there looking at my reflection in the store window.

"Hey, kid. Why aren't you in school?" said someone coming up from behind me.

When I looked up, it was a police officer. I knew at that moment, it was time to go back to the prison. As usual, I spent the next two weeks in the Juvenile Shelter, before I was taken back to the Children's Home Society Orphanage.

About three months later, I broke into the clothing room and stole my new clothes, and then ran away again. I searched for two days trying to find the man's house. All I could remember was that it was over by the hospital. When I did find the house, there was no one there.

"Can I help you?" asked the neighbor.

"I'm looking for the man and woman who live right here," I said, pointing at the house.

"They no longer live there," the man told me.

"Do you know where they went?"

"You related to them?"

"I don't know what that related means," I told him.

"Look here, boy. Judy died of cancer several months back, and then old Carl… well, he shot himself a couple of days later."

I reached into my pocket, took out a cigarette, and lit it with a match. When I opened my mouth to speak, a large smoke ring came out. I stood there watching it as it circled around my head.

"It looks like you're all dressed up with nowhere to go?" said the man.

I turned around and walked back to the orphanage. I did not run away again for more than a year. I did not have any place left to go.

Memories

I had been missing for three days, and I knew that the police were once again looking for me, just as they had every other time that I ran away from the orphanage. It was early November, and it was starting to turn cold during the evening hours. Generally, when we boys ran away we would head to one of the local parks to hide. While in the park, men would approach us, the kind of men who like to take young boys to their house.

I was eleven years old, and I had known about these "queer" men for almost three years now. Being with them was the only way orphan boys could survive out on the streets of Jacksonville. This particular time, I had run away all by myself, and I have to admit I was very scared, especially when darkness fell. I did not know anyone, what to do, or where to turn for help.

It was about eight o'clock in the evening when I finally made my way over to the Springfield area. Most of the people now walking the streets were bums, drunks and prostitutes. I made my way down a small alley, and found a large cardboard box next to a dumpster. I took off my flannel shirt, and made a pillow out of it. I put my coat over my T-shirt, and climbed inside the box, trying to hide and get some sleep.

"You come out here. Get out of that box, boy!" someone yelled, as he began to hit the top of the box with something hard.

I stuck my head out of the end of the box, and looked around.

"What you got there, boy?" asked an old man.

I could tell that he had been drinking, because I could smell it all over him.

"I ain't got anything. Really, I don't," I replied.

"You got something there, boy. I seen it in your hand when you climbed in that box," he said, as he moved closer to me.

"It's just a letter and a picture. I ain't got any money. Honest, I don't."

I began pushing myself backwards away from him, until my back was against the brick wall of the building.

I ain't going to hurt you boy. Just want to look at what you got there," said the scary old man.

Slowly, I climbed out of the somewhat collapsed cardboard box, and held the letter out to the man. He took it from my hand. I followed him as he walked over to the large fire, which he and several other men had made in a large metal drum. I stood watching his face as he read the contents of the letter. After he finished, he opened the envelope and took out the small picture of my mother.

"Nice looking woman. Is this your mother?" he asked me.

"That's what Henry R. Trusty said in the letter," I told him.

"Who's this Trusty fellow, and where do you live?" he asked.

"He's my grandpa, and he lives in Alaska," I replied. "When I ain't running away, I live at the Children's Home Orphanage on San Diego Road. That's over by Spring Park School."

"If you know what's good for you kid, you will tear up that damn picture. Just throw it in the fire-can, and go back to the orphanage where you belong. If your momma really wanted you, then she would not have put you in the orphanage in the first place. You're going to see that one day, boy."

"How do you know what's good? You're just drunk all the time; I can smell it."

"Look here, kid. I was raised in a rat-hole orphanage up in Chicago. I have to admit that those nuns were some terrible bitches. But at least we got fed every day, and they taught us some learning," said the man, as he poked his finger in my face.

You were an orphan one time, too?" I asked the man.

He shook his head back and forth, and then took a long drink from the bottle that he had wrapped in a brown paper sack.

"Damn, that bites hard," he said, as he began choking and coughing.

"Leave the kid alone, and stop trying to scare the hell out of him," said a woman, as she walked up to the barrel and began warming her hands.

I watched the woman as she placed her hands directly into the flames. As she talked, she constantly turned her hands back and forth so they would not burn in the fire.

"Just telling the kid the damn truth of it all. This is no place for his kind," he told the woman.

"How come your hands don't burn?" I asked the woman.

"It's magic, sonny," she told me, as she laughed out loud. "Get up here and warm yourself."

Then she wrapped her arm around my neck.

"I got a kid that's about your age. Don't know where he is any more," she said, as she hugged me.

I watched her face in the firelight, as she swallowed and wiped her face on her skirt tail.

"This is not a place for you boy. Really, it ain't, " she said in a broken voice. "Give me a shot of that poke," she ordered the old man, as she punched him in the arm.

"You want to snort?" asked the short, bald man.

"Don't be giving none of that damn shit to that boy!" screamed the lady.

"I was going to buy him a Coca Cola."

"Would you like a Coke, young man?" he asked.

"Yes, sir," I replied.

"Did you hear that? The boy called me a 'yes, sir'."

Off walked the man heading to the store located down the block.

"I love all children," said the woman, as she hugged me even tighter. "You warm enough?"

"Yes, ma'am."

"Here boy, eat some of this jerky. It's good for ya," said the man, who had remained very quiet.

For the next hour or two, I stood around the fire eating beef jerky and drinking Coca Colas. The five of us talked, laughed, and sang a few songs. The more they drank, the more they hugged on me. Occasionally, the old drunk woman would kiss me on the cheek. Sometimes when she would hug me, it would hurt my neck very badly. However, that was okay with me. It felt very good to be around people who treated me as if I was somebody special. It was good to be around someone who did not make me work all the time, as the orphanage did. In addition, it was very good to be around grown-up people who did not want me to take my clothes off for them.

"You had best get back in that box and get some sleep. Morning comes early round here," said the lady.

I warmed my backside, and then headed back over to the box. I placed my flannel shirt beneath my head and within minutes, I was fast asleep.

"Okay, boy!" yelled someone, as he kicked my feet.

I quickly sat up and tried to figure out where I was. But nothing made any sense to me.

"Come on, boy. Crawl it out here," said a man's voice.

When I looked up, there were two police officers standing at my feet. One of them kept hitting me on the bottom of my shoes.

"Hurry it up," said the officer.

As I stood up, the two men grabbed me by my arms, and headed me toward their patrol car.

Sorry, kid. I had to call them. It's for the best," said the woman, as we walked by her.

I sat in the back of the police car for about thirty minutes, while the police officers took a report from the woman. Occasionally, she would look over and wave at me. I was not very happy about having to go back to the orphanage. However, I was not worried about that right now. All that I could think about was that it felt good for someone to like me, even if it was only for an hour or two.

Those few memories have stayed with me through the years. Those memories taught me that there are good, kind people everywhere in the world. Even in the back alleys of America.

Skin That Nigger

This was one of the few times when I had run away from the orphanage by myself. I just could not take going to school any longer. I walked right passed the school without even looking. I threw my schoolbooks in the bushes, and off I walked down Spring Park Road.

I could not understand why the other children in our school hated us kids from the Children's Home Society Orphanage, or why they always made fun of us. Was it because we didn't have lunch money, and carried our sandwich in a brown paper bag? What had we ever done to them? Why did they always find it necessary to laugh and make fun of us?

Five days a week, we went to school, and then we went back to the orphanage, and worked until bedtime. It was the same routine every day, year after year. On Saturdays and Sundays, we scrubbed and waxed all the floors, and the two stairways. Then we cleaned all the toilets and sinks in the bathrooms, kitchen and washrooms. Whatever daylight was left, we spent raking acres and acres of leaves and pine straw. Then we placed it in the azalea beds.

Several times, I had thought about killing myself, but I was just too scared to do something like that. I thought about asking some of the other boys who were really sad and lonely to do it with me. But I was afraid that they might report me to Mother Winter's, the head matron. I do not think she really cared if I died one way or the other. One time, she told me that she would kill me. I was staring at her face when she said that, and I think she really meant it. The veins in her face were real big and blue, and her eyes were coming out of her head a little bit.

"So today I'm just going to go to wherever somewhere is," I thought to myself, as I slowly walked along the side of the road.

I walked over the Main Street Bridge, and headed into downtown Jacksonville. Generally, when I had run away, the orphanage would call the police, and I would have to run when they found me. This time, I just did not seem to care. As I walked around looking in the department store windows, I thought about what had happened the night before—how Mother Winters had called my dormitory houseparent, and had me report to her room at the dining room building. When I arrived, I knew from the look on her face that I was not in trouble. I sat down on the end of her bed, and folded my hands on my lap. I stared at the floor and began to swing my legs back and forth. I sat there listening to her hum, as she began to shower.

"Roger, dear. Hand me that robe on the end of my bed," she hollered.

"Yes, ma'am, Mother Winters."

I reached over, picked up the long, white robe, and handed it to her through the crack in the doorway. When

I turned around, I noticed all the horse statues lined up in a row. I had given her one almost every Christmas. Every penny that I had ever received at Christmas from the Jacksonville Kiwanis Club had been spent buying the pretty ceramic horses for Mother Winters. God! How much I wanted her to like me.

"Roger, dear. Did you take a shower tonight?"

"No, ma'am, Mother Winters. It wasn't shower time yet. We were still watching the television."

I jumped when she opened the bathroom door. Her robe was open, and I could see the front of her body. She walked up to me and opened her robe further. She gently sat me down on the end of her bed, took my head in both her hands, and placed it against her breasts. I closed my eyes, and waited for her to masturbate. It was the exact same routine every time.

"I wonder if she is ever going to make me do it to her. I'm eleven, and I ain't never really done it," I thought to myself, as I crossed over the street.

I walked around for hours. There were times when I did not even know where I was in Jacksonville. It really did not matter where I was, so I just kept walking. As the sun slowly disappeared behind the trees, I began to wonder what I was going to do for the night. My legs were tired, and I needed to find a place to rest. I sat down on a city bus bench for just a moment, but jumped right back up when I saw a bus turn the corner. The bus pulled up and came to a stop. When the door opened, I stood there looking at the bus driver. I did not know what to do.

"Well," he said.

I was very embarrassed, and did not want to get into trouble. Having several dollars in my pocket I stepped on and paid the toll. Then I took a seat in the rear of the bus. I continued to ride for several hours, falling asleep and waking each time the bus would come to a stop. After about another hour, there was no one on the bus except the driver and me. I noticed that he kept looking at me in the rearview mirror, so I decided to get off. I reached up and pulled the cord, making the bell ring. The bus came to a stop, and I exited through the back door. I choked on the exhaust as the bus pulled away.

It was very dark, and I had no idea where I was. Off in the distance, I could hear a train whistle, so I began to walk in that direction. Several minutes later, I came to what appeared to be a train yard. There were train tracks everywhere. I stood there wondering if I might be able to sleep in one of the many empty boxcars parked along the track. As I walked down the tracks, several men began shouting at me. When I did not move, they ran toward me. I spun around, and began running in the opposite direction. Within five minutes, the two men had cornered me beneath the railroad overpass. One of them grabbed me by the shirt, hit me with his flashlight, and threw me to the ground.

"Hey, there's another one over here," yelled the second man.

I was surprised when the man pulled out a gun and pointed it at me.

"This one over here is a nigger."

"Bring him over here!" hollered the man, while holding me at gunpoint.

"This is the same bastard we ran out of here last night," said the man, as he reached our location.

I looked at the black man, and saw that he was scared to death. He was shaking so badly that he could hardly walk.

"What did I tell you last night, boy?"

"You'se said you would skin me alive, if I ever came back here," said the man.

"Let's skin that nigger," said the man holding onto me.

"How old are you, boy?"

"Eleven," I replied.

"You get your little ass out of here, and don't you ever come back.

You understand?"

"Yes, sir!" I said, and I meant it.

The man loosened his grip, and I slowly moved away from him. Then I turned and started walking in the direction of the tracks.

"Not that way! That way!"

The man stuck out his finger and pointed.

"I'm lost, and I don't know where I am."

"That-a-way!" he screamed.

I began walking backwards away from them. After about twenty feet, I stopped.

"Move!" he yelled.

"What are you going to do to him?" I asked the two men.

"I am going to skin this here black bastard."

"Please do not hurt him. I'll take him away with me, really I will."

I watched as one of the men flashed a large Bowie knife into the beam of his flashlight.

"Please let him go. He ain't hurt anybody," I pleaded.

The two men grabbed the black man and threw him to the ground.

"Oh, God! Oh, God!" I screamed.

The black man rose to his knees, and began begging for his life. The two men began laughing, and one kicked the man back to the ground with his foot. I just sat there on the ground, shaking and crying.

"Here, take this damned monkey with you," said one of the men, as he continued to laugh.

I tried to get up, but I could hardly walk. I crawled through the dirt on my knees. When I reached the man, I helped him to his feet. He and I began to run, holding onto each other. We must have fallen ten times, before we got fifty feet away from the two men. The black man was screaming like a crazy person. Even after we were far away, he was still shaking, and acting as if he was not right inside his head.

That night, he and I slept behind South Gate Plaza over on the south side of Jacksonville. We found refuge on two old couches that someone had dumped behind one of the stores. Late the next morning when I woke, the black man was gone. I sat there on that old couch for several hours, wondering if those two men would have really skinned a human being alive.

My mind was very confused. I was searching for a place in the world that had to be better than the world that I lived in at the orphanage. No matter where I looked, I just could not find that world.

The Baby

When daylight arrived, it was necessary for me to stay off the main streets of Jacksonville, mainly because the police were looking for me. On this morning, it was raining very hard, making it difficult for me to move from one location to another. My nights were generally spent in the parks, and during the daytime, I would move to one of several abandoned red brick buildings located on Riverside Avenue, along the banks of the St. John's River.

I walked through the knee-high weeds, and entered the old building from the east side. Stepping over large wooden planks and empty boxes, I began to shake my hands, trying to sling some of the water off myself. I was soaked to the bone. I started to unbutton my shirt, when I heard someone talking at the other end of the building. I quickly ducked down behind one of the many wooden posts that held the old structure upright.

"This is my hideout. What are you doing in here?" I thought to myself, as I once again began to listen.

"Well, I don't know what we are going to do!" screamed a man's voice.

All at once, a baby began to cry. With eyes opened wide, I stretched my neck around the side of the large post to see if I could tell what was happening at the other end of the building. The only light coming in the building was from the outside. There were many windows, but they were way high up. A few were broken, but most were dirty, blocking whatever light might come in. It was very hard for me to see anything.

"Shut the little bastard up, or I'll ring its damn neck," said the man.

"Please don't hurt my baby," said a woman's voice.

Slowly, on my hands and knees, I moved along the dirty floor making my way toward the sounds. The baby cried, and it cried, and it cried. It just would not quit. I stopped and hid behind a stack of old tires when I thought that I was about thirty feet from where they might be hiding. All at once, a flock of pigeons flew across from one rafter to another, causing me to jump.

"Who's there?" yelled the man as he stood up.

Carefully, I stood up, and faced in his direction.

"What you doing in here?" he asked.

"I'm here a lot when I need a place to stay."

"Shut that god-damn baby up!" screamed the man to the girl sitting at his feet.

"Why you in here with a baby? Ain't you got a place to live?" I questioned.

"My baby was just born last night," said the young girl.

"You had a baby in here?"

She nodded her head, telling me "yes."

"Ain't people supposed to go to the hospital to have a baby?"

The man sat back down on the dirty floor. No one said a word. I walked over and stood there looking at the woman who was holding the baby in her arms. All at once, she pulled up her T-shirt exposing her large breasts.

"God! I ain't never seen girls' titties that big before. They look like they might bust, they're so big," I thought to myself.

The woman took the baby, and began to nurse it. Even when feeding, the baby kept making funny sounds. Sort of like a puppy makes when it is scratching, and cannot get a flea to stop biting.

"Well, we have got to get out of here. Feed the damn thing and throw it in the damn river," said the man.

The girl reached down and kissed the baby on the top of its head.

"He can't really mean that. Nobody would throw a little baby in the river, would they?" I wondered.

I stood there for more than five minutes. Neither of them said another word to me. Finally, I turned around, walked back to my end of the building, and sat down in the corner. Now and then, I would hear the man yell at the girl, and then all would become quiet once more. It must have been half an hour, before the baby began to cry again. Once again, the man began to scream trying to shut the baby up. The next thing I knew, the man was walking toward me, holding the baby in his arms. It was screaming at the top of its lungs. He kept walking closer and closer to where I was sitting. Then he stopped directly in front of me, and just stood there, staring into my eyes.

Quickly, he turned and walked out the side door of the building. I stood up and walked to the opening, hoping to see what he was doing. All at once, someone grabbed me on the shoulder. When I spun around, I saw the girl was gasping for air and unable to breathe. I began slapping her on the back until she caught her breath.

"He's going to kill my baby."

I looked out the large opening, and saw the man standing at the edge of the river, but I did not see the baby in his arms. I ran toward him as fast as I could. When I reached him, I saw the baby lying on the ground beside him. Out of breath, I sat down on the ground and opened the dirty towel wrapped around the child. I took off my undershirt, and used spit trying to clean the dried blood off the baby's face and arms. It looked so helpless.

Though only eleven years old, I had run away from the orphanage many times in the last five years. By traveling the streets and back alleys of Jacksonville, I had learned much about survival. I knew that one had to be very careful, and he had best not get anyone mad at him. I sat there wondering. Should I tell the man I would call the police, if he tried to throw the baby into the river?

"Surely, he would beat me, or try to choke me to death, like one queer guy tried to do several weeks before," I thought.

"If you don't want it, can I have it?" I asked the man.

"Have what?"

"That little baby."

"What would you do with a god-damn baby?" he asked.

"I'll take it back to the orphanage with me. It is better to be in the orphanage, than to be dead. Right?" I blurted out.

I could hardly believe those words came out of my mouth. As bad as the orphanage was, I realized looking in that baby's face that being dead was far worse than being molested, mistreated, and going hungry. The man stood there looking out over the river. I looked up and saw the girl walking toward him. She walked up behind him, placed her arms around his waist, and the two of them just stood there, silently. I stood, picked the baby up off the ground, and waited for the man to reply. Slowly, I began to walk backwards into the tall weeds.

"Don't you say anything about where that baby came from, you hear?" said the man.

"Yes, sir."

I watched the two of them as I continued to walk backwards. When I reached the sidewalk, more than 200 yards away, neither one of them had even turned around to look at me. I carried the baby to the city park over by Five Points. I sat on the bench for about an hour, rocking the baby back and forth. Soon it began to cry, and I could not get it to stop. I took the baby into a local store, and asked one of the women if she had something that I could feed it.

As the word spread that I had found the baby lying in the park, a large crowd began to gather. Within ten or fifteen minutes, there were people everywhere. While everyone was looking at the baby, I filled my pockets with candy bars and penny candy. Then I slipped out the door, and back out into the world I traveled.

Our Friends – The Police

Here I was again, a runaway with nothing to call my own, and facing the long night ahead. Then, straight ahead, looming in the twilight, I saw it. Shabby, falling down, no glass in the windows, boards missing here and there, but it had a door. Hey, looked like a good place to sleep for the night. I walked around the abandoned house, and entered through the opening, which at one time must have had a door. I smiled, and was glad to have found shelter before dark.

A young boy living on the streets has to be careful, you know. I had newfound freedom that I enjoyed, but I needed protection by hiding out, being ever watchful not to be seen, and at all costs, avoiding the orphanage matron and the police. For a boy who had run away many times, always looking for a place "somewhere over the rainbow," I was rather sure that I still had not found it.

It was dark inside, and smelled of piss, rotten garbage, and vomit. It took a moment for my eyes to adjust to the light, and when they did, it hit home. This was one God-awful filthy place. What I had smelled was indeed on the floor, along with roaches, rats and moldy, rotten "whatever" lumps here and there. However, it still served me well for the moment. I figured I could maybe clean it up fairly good. After all, at the orphanage, I was known as the best toilet cleaner ever to grace the place.

I walked around the room taking it all in, sizing it all up, and feeling proud of myself for my discovery. All of a sudden, from somewhere deep within the darkness, I heard the far away murmur of voices. I was not alone!

"Maybe it was a ghost. Maybe someone lives here after all," I thought.

I began to inch down the darkened hallway, thinking I could sneak up on them and have a look.

"Best be real cautious," I kept thinking.

I had learned early on not to trust anybody; grownups just were not good people. I followed the hallway, stepping around tin cans, old wooden planks, and hundreds of beer bottles. The further I got into the old house, the more terrified I became. I might not be able to escape, which scared me even more. As I moved forward, the voices were getting louder and louder with every step.

I crept up to a doorway and peeked in. I saw four men drinking and smoking cigarettes. Without warning, a hand grabbed the back of my shirt, and propelled me into the room. I raised my hands as though I were ready to fight.

"Hey, boys! Look here what we got. Caught the little shit hiding by the door, spying on us. Guess we should teach him what we do to spies."

"Hey, it's that little bastard from down by the bus station. What are you doing here? You follow us here?"

I put my hands down when I recognized two of the men.

"You know this kid?" asked the man who had grabbed me in the hallway.

"We know him. He ran down to the liquor store for us a couple of times to get us some wine. One of them damn farts from the orphanage over on the south side."

"What's the matter, boy? Cat got your tongue?"

"I ain't no bastard. I just ain't got no place to live," I replied.

"Hey, hear that! He ain't got no place to go. Let him stay here. He can fetch water, and clean the damn place up. You got any other uses?"

They all began to laugh, point at me, and shake their heads.

"Something smells bad, like something dead," I blurted out.

"Well, dip shit, it's that damn dog over there in the corner. Been dead for two days. You do not like the smell, then that is your first job. Get your little ass over there, and tote that dog outside."

I looked over in the corner, and saw the dead dog. Its coat was all covered in crusting blood.

"I can't carry no dog that big."

They all laughed, waved their hands in the air, and promptly turned their backs on me. I stood there for five minutes, ignored by everyone. I finally walked over and took a seat in the corner, trying to make my body as small as possible. For hours, they sat drinking and smoking. Several of them walked over and pissed on the wall in the corner of the room every now and then.

The orphanage was bad, but not like this. It was hard to believe people lived like this. They smelled so bad that I held my nose when they came near me. Their hair was shiny and matted, as if it had grease in it. Some of them had sores, and every one of them was continually scratching. They scratched their heads, their arms, their legs, and even between their legs.

I stayed for about two weeks, just hanging out and trying to stay out of their way. I cleaned up the house as well as I could, but it didn't do any good. Every day, the living room filled up with cans and bottles. When I would sit down to rest, someone would throw a bottle against the wall to break it, and then make me clean it up. As there was no electricity, gas or water, one of my daily jobs was to haul five-gallon buckets of water from the spigot behind the paint store.

There was no food in the house, and what food they did bring home was stolen. I was terribly hungry most of the time, but I dared not ask for much of anything. I stole what I could when they were not looking, but I was not very successful. Someone always seemed to miss what little food I had taken. They would sneer and threaten me. Several times, they made me listen to a five-minute speech about what they did to "little bastards" who stole from them. As an eleven-year-old boy from an orphanage, I might not have had much smarts. But it always seemed strange to me that these people had money for liquor and cigarettes, but never for food.

In the time I was there, all they really wanted to do was sit around drinking, smoking, cussing and telling dirty jokes. So I fetched the water, and went to the liquor store for liquor or cigarettes. I never let my guard down, and I stayed away from them as much as I could. I felt much safer that way.

Deep down in my gut, I knew these were bad people, and I knew that I should not be there. But even that was better than the orphanage. There, I was at least somebody who got to work, and go get stuff for them. Back at the orphanage, I was nobody, nobody at all.

I had pretty well gotten used to the routine, and felt more comfortable being able to stay there. However, soon it was all going to come crashing down on me. It was a terrible night, in a horrible place, with the cruelest people I have ever known. About two o'clock in the morning, I was awakened suddenly, and all hell was breaking loose around me. People were screaming and yelling; there were flashlight beams bouncing off bodies, walls, the ceiling and the floor.

A hand grabbed the back of my shirt, taking some of my skin with it. The front of my shirt strangled me like a noose. I was yanked, first one way and then another, then hit over and over with a flashlight. Someone kicked me in the stomach and the back, and then threw me to the floor like a rag doll. All around me, people were screaming and yelling as if they were being beaten to death. The sound of bones crushing was loud enough to be heard above the cries for help. I felt a hand grab my leg, and realized that I was being dragged out of the room. Down the hallway I slid, and then was being shoved down the stairs. My head, back, arms and ribs felt every blow as I bounced off each stair like a rubber ball.

"I thought policemen were supposed to be our friends!" I yelled, as I was body-slammed down the stairs.

"Shut up you little tramp," was the only reply.

At the bottom of the stairs, the kicks and hitting began again. I curled up tight to protect myself from the blows, but it did no good. The police officer seemed enraged, and he just kept hitting me over and over and over. I was sure that I was going to die before he stopped beating me. Then it was over as quickly as it had started. They just stopped. The police came and the police went. They arrested no one, and they helped no one. They just left us for dead, like that dog in the corner of the room I had seen only weeks before.

I stumbled around in the darkness, going first in one direction, then another, always led by the sounds of crying and the gasps of pain. I started a small fire from the newspapers that had been stacked in the corner. I could hardly believe my eyes when I saw tons of blood all over the walls and floor. Most of them, women included, had been beaten senseless. Many of them had bloody noses, gashes on their heads, and numerous cuts and bruises. I looked at my arms, and then ran my hands over my head. I felt the whelps rising on my head, and I hurt so badly. I was numb all over, and could not cry. At that very moment, I felt nothing.

In the orphanage, they told me that I was a nothing, but I did not know what it really felt like to be "a nothing" until now. I knew the cops were not my friends, but I didn't know they hated people so much, especially boys.

I went over to one of the men and asked, "Why did they do that?"

His only reply was, "It's what you get when you're a bum, kid. That is life on the streets. Get out of here right now, and go back where you came from. If you're smart, you won't come around here again."

I walked downstairs and into the living room, and picked up a bag of potato chips. I took them, but for the first time, I was not hungry. I just held on to them for dear life, for they were all I had to carry away from that place. I walked to a corner drug store and asked the man if I could use his telephone. He looked at me, but never asked about why I was bleeding. He allowed me to use the phone, but he made no effort to help me. He just simply turned his back and walked away.

I called for an ambulance to help the people in the house. I waited and waited, but no help ever came. I walked out of the store, and stood motionless on the street corner. I began to eat the chips, before someone came along and took them away from me. I looked up at the stars and wondered why the world was such a shitty place.

"A shitty place," I kept saying to myself, over and over.

I guess I was no longer innocent to the cruelty. It was not just the orphanage; it was everywhere, from everybody. Slowly, I began walking south toward the orphanage. When I got back, they saw that I had been severely beaten. Nevertheless, they beat the hell out of me again. It made no difference to me anyway. Whether it was the orphanage or the streets; I had learned that bastards come in all sizes and shapes, and that the cops, who were supposed to be the good guys, were just as bad as the bums.

The Magic Letter

Once again, I had run away, and really do not know why. I would walk out the gate to go to school, and then keep walking, and walking, and walking. I had just turned eleven years old the week before. It was almost dark; I was tired, scared, cold, and all alone. I had not eaten all day, and was afraid to turn myself in to the police. I knew I would receive another beating once I returned to the Children's Home Society in Jacksonville, Florida. There was nothing for me to do, except keep on walking.

As darkness fell, I made my way over to the city park located on Park Street. I entered the darkened area, and sat down on one of the wooden benches, hoping to avoid the police cars. It was cold, and I began to shiver uncontrollably. All was quiet, except for the passing cars in the distance.

"Well, hello, young man," a voice came from behind me.

I jumped, almost falling off the park bench. My heart was beating ninety miles per hour, and I could feel it thumping in the side of my neck. I gasped, and I could hardly catch my breath. I looked up, and saw a woman standing behind me in the shadows.

"You look cold," she said.

"I'm cold. I'm real, real cold." I continued to shiver.

"Here wrap this around you."

I watched as she took off her shawl, and wrapped it around my shoulders.

"But ain't you gonna be cold now?"

"I'll be ok."

"Is there anything else you need?" she questioned.

"I sure could use some food."

"Follow me," she said.

I walked with her about twenty feet, then she stopped under one of the park streetlights.

She held out her hand and said, "Here, you take this letter, and give it to the store owner."

I looked at her outstretched arm, but saw nothing in her hand. "There's nothing in your hand," I told her.

"Roger, reach out and take the letter from my hand," she replied.

Slowly I reached out, acting as though I was taking something from her hand.

"Now close your thumb and finger, and hold the paper tightly," she instructed.

I closed my thumb and finger as though I were grasping the letter.

"Take it to any store owner."

"What do I say to them?"

"Nothing," she replied.

"But what store do I go to?"

"It doesn't matter," she said, as she smiled.

I turned and began walking toward Five Points. Several blocks down the road, I came to a store with a woman sitting behind a counter. I opened the door, walked in, and stopped directly in front of her.

"Can I help you?" asked the woman.

I was hesitant to talk, and had no idea what I should say. Very slowly I held out my hand toward her. I watched her face to see if she might think I was crazy or something.

"Is that for me?" she asked.

"Yes, ma'am." I looked down at the floor.

She reached out, and as her hand touched mine, I opened my tightly closed fingers, and stood there waiting. She pulled back, smiled, and looked down at her hands.

She immediately turned, and walked to the back of the store. I began to inch toward the front door, for fear she might be calling the police. Just as I made it to the front door, I stopped as I heard someone call my name. I turned around, and saw the woman holding a paper plate.

"Roger, here is something for you to eat."

"How did you know my name?" I asked her.

"It was on the paper."

"But there wasn't no paper. I didn't see no paper," I told her.

She smiled, and motioned for me to eat by twirling her finger in front of her mouth. Within two or three minutes, I had downed the entire plate of food, and several Coca Colas.

"Are you full?" she asked.

"Yes, ma'am."

"Then it's time for you to go."

I turned to leave when I felt her hand on my shoulder.

"Here, your paper. You almost forgot your letter," she said, holding out her hand.

Again, seeing nothing, I held out my hand and closed my thumb and finger as though I were taking something from her. Tightly grasping nothing more than air, I walked out into the street, and headed back to the park. When I arrived, the old woman was sitting on the park bench. "Did you eat?" she asked.

"Yes, ma'am, and I had two Coca Colas, too."

"Good."

"How do you do that magic?" I asked her.

"It's not magic."

"But how does everyone know my name?"

"It is written in the letter."

"Can I have the letter so I can be magic too?" I asked.

She reached out, took my hand, and opened my tightly closed fingers. Whatever was being held between my fingers, she took and placed into her apron pocket. "Would you help someone if they were hungry or lost?" she asked me.

"Yes, ma'am."

"Would you help someone if they were hurt, cold or scared?"

"Yes, ma'am. I would be their best friend."

"Roger, you are a very kind and lucky little boy. Because of that you will never need to use the magic letter," she responded.

She stood up, kissed me on the forehead, removed the shawl from my shoulders, and began walking down the sidewalk. I watched as she disappeared into the darkness.

A Ghost?

It was an unusual feeling, looking back at the orphanage gates, and knowing that we would never have to return there. Wayne Evers and I had once again decided that we were old enough, at the age of eleven and twelve, to take off and start a new life of our own. It was also a scary feeling leaving the security of the fences of the orphanage. As bad as the beatings were on us kids, I guess we felt that no one in the outside world could hurt us as badly as did the matrons at the orphanage.

When ten or fifteen of us would run away together, it was not so bad. However, with only the two of us, there were just not enough eyes to look out for the many dangers we had heard about. After all, there were the orphanage people who would be after us, as well as the police. We knew that there were plenty of bad people out there in the world who would hurt us.

Once again having nothing to eat, we decided to drop by the Patio Restaurant and get one last cache of food, candy and cigarettes to take on our long journey out into the new world. It had been several months since we boys had been caught illegally entering the Patio Restaurant. Therefore, we were quite sure that it would be safe to enter just one last time. We'd take only what we really needed to survive, until we could each get a job, and maybe a place of our own.

When leaving the restaurant, we had cleaned up our mess, and placed all the empty candy wrappers into the garbage can, as well as replaced all the glass in the back window. We had taken only what we really needed to survive, which was about fifteen candy bars, ten bags of potato chips, and five cartons of cigarettes each.

We walked over to the old Spanish house, an abandoned house on the south side of Jacksonville. It was near the orphanage, and was a hideout for kids who ran away from home, orphan or not. When we arrived, we found that there were about ten unknown people staying there, so we headed out to find our own place. We walked for about two hours, and had finally decided to try this old, abandoned white house that we had heard about over by Landon Junior and Senior High School.

It was a very scary-looking place. It was a big, two-story white building with almost all the glass broken out of the windows. We sat outside in the dark for the longest time talking about the old house, and if the place might be haunted, or have ghosts inside. It sure was a scary-looking old building. However, after careful consideration, it was determined between our two brilliant minds, that there were no such things as ghosts. We would make this our new home. After all, no one really wanted the old house, or it would have been taken care of.

We forced open the front door, and entered the pitch-black house. We lit a match, and immediately saw a large staircase to our right, leading to the upstairs. As we started up the stairs, they began to creak, so we stopped dead in our tracks. We once again began discussing the possibilities of ghosts and various creatures of the night. We stood motionless for about five minutes, lighting one match after another. We wanted to make sure that there were no ghosts waiting for us at the top of the stairs.

When we reached the landing, we were just about out of matches. Our fingers were burnt from holding the matches for as long as possible. When we reached the top of the stairs, it was pitch dark, and neither Wayne nor I could even see each other. I took the last match from the pack and struck it, holding it high into the air.

"There is a big bed in here," said Wayne.

Just about that time, someone large sat straight up in the bed, and pointed a rifle at us.

"Bang!" went the gun as it fired.

I heard the bullet hit the wall next to my head. I shoved Wayne as hard as I could toward the landing. Then down the staircase we went, rolling head over heals.

"Bang! Bang! Bang!" went the rifle, as it continued to fire in our direction.

Out the door and down the railroad tracks we ran as fast as we could. I was one of the fastest runners in the orphanage, but this time, Wayne passed me screaming like a maniac. It never entered my head that the individual shooting at us was a human being. All I could think about was that there was a darned ghost shooting at me, and that it was going to catch and kill me. By the time we stopped running, all our cigarettes, candy bars and potato chips, which had been tucked into the belly of our shirts, had all been strewn along at least 200 miles of railroad tracks. Well, actually it was about half a mile, but it seemed like 200 miles.

Late that night, we returned to the orphanage and climbed into our warm beds, and the orphanage was never the wiser. I think that was the week that I decided to get baptized at the Swain Memorial Methodist Church in Jacksonville, Florida.

God knows I needed it!

I guess it was several weeks before I began to think about, or even start to realize what had actually happened that night. I finally understood just how dangerous that situation really was, and how close the two of us came to losing our lives.

Hungry For Diamonds

I had run away from the orphanage once again, at the age of twelve. This time it was because the matron had told one of the smaller boys she was going to "cut his wee-wee off" with scissors, if he wet his bed again.

Well, I got up one morning, and went in to use the bathroom. I found Ronnie sitting in the corner of the shower sobbing his eyes out. No matter what I said, I could not get him to stop crying.

I walked back to his bedroom, found that his sheets were lying on the floor, and they had been burned. I ran back to the large bathroom and asked him how his sheets got on fire. He told me that he had wet the bed. Then he had gone into one of the older boy's lockers, and had taken some matches. The older boys used them for smoking cigarette butts that they stole out of one of the women's cars who worked at the office. He had tried to dry his sheets using the matches, but the one sheet caught on fire, and he had to stick it into the toilet to get the fire out.

I knew that this four-year-old kid was as good as dead when the matron found out what he had done. I told him to go to his bedroom and get his clothes and shoes on; we were going to go away, and I would make sure that he would not be beaten, nor have his wee-wee cut off.

Within fifteen minutes, we had scaled the oak tree outside my bedroom window, and were heading down San Diego Road to who-knows-where.

We managed to hitchhike several rides from different people. We finally made it to St. Augustine, Florida. I managed to steal some apples from a store, so we could eat. I made sure that little Ronnie did not see me steal the apples, because I did not want him to grow up and become "a no-good thief" like me. That is what the orphanage always called me after I was caught fishing in a man's goldfish pond, and for eating his pears off his fruit trees. We walked around for several hours wondering where to go.

All of a sudden, this strange man came walking up to us, and asked us if we wanted a job selling magazines. I told him I would sell his magazines if my little Ronnie could stay with me. He said that was okay. He took us to a really big street with lots of nice homes, and told us to go from door to door, then to let the people fill out the papers. They would give us some money, and we were to bring the money back to him at his car. Most of the people got very mad at me for coming up to their house and for knocking on their door. I did not like them yelling at me like that. So, I told the man that I did not want to sell his magazines any more. He put the two of us in his car and took us for a hamburger, and told us that he would take us to a new place where the people would not be so mean.

After he dropped us off at the new street, I decided to try something different. I took a piece of paper and wrote a note telling the people that I was deaf and dumb. I would walk up to their house, knock on the front door and hand them the note I had written. Then I would talk while biting down on my tongue making it sound like I was crazy, stupid or something. Talking like that made me sound just like I was crazy, and no one got mad again. They would just smile at me when I talked, and I would hand them the paper for the magazines. I think people liked me better when I was stupid.

Within several hours, I had collected almost $80, and the man started hugging me when we got back to his car. He asked me if we wanted to go to Miami with him. He said we could make lots of money in Miami, and we could stay in a big hotel. So off we went in his big, old fancy car, just the three of us. We arrived in big Miami late that night, and he got us a room at the Hawaiian Isles Motel. I will never forget the name of that fancy place. It had a swimming pool, and he said it was where all the rich people stayed. However, I did not see any fancy people staying there at all—just plain-old-looking people like us.

We made Mike lots of money every day, but he would never give us any of it. All we ever had to eat was one hamburger at nighttime when we gave him all the money. I did take some of the money one time, to buy us a Coke. Oh yeah, and I did buy us some ice cream once from a man on a bicycle. That thing had a freezer on the front of it. Every day, we would really get hungry, and could hardly wait to get back to the motel for our hamburger. One day, we had made lots of money, so I took my friend Ronnie into a drug store. We bought a sandwich and a whole bunch of candy bars. Boy, was that man mad when he found out what we had done. He pushed me down on the ground, and then slapped little Ronnie across the face as hard as he could.

Late that same night when everyone was asleep, I woke Ronnie. We snuck out of that motel room, and we ran away. We lived on the beach for two days without anything to eat, not even our one hamburger. Finally, I went to a restaurant and asked a man for some money. I had decided to call the orphanage and tell them where we were, because we were so hungry. He gave me a dollar, and I walked to the back room to use the telephone. I dialed the "O" for the operator, and asked her for the number of the orphanage in Jacksonville. However, she did not know what I was talking about, and told me to hold on for a minute. While I was waiting for her to come back on the phone, I saw a big freezer right next to me. I reached over and opened one of the big white doors. Inside were hundreds of hamburger patties with paper between each one. I hung up the phone and grabbed about ten of the hamburgers, and put them down the front of my pants, which did not feel real good, 'cause they were really cold. I walked out of the restaurant real fast and stiff-legged like, and we headed back down to the beach.

When we got to the beach, we started gathering firewood to build a fire to cook the raw hamburgers. We were hungry and our stomachs were hurting very badly. After we got a fire, we tried to hold the hamburgers over the heat, but it was just too hot, and we could not hold onto them. I decided to walk up to the back of the motel to see if I could find something to cook on, like a piece of old metal. However, I found nothing for us to use. As I looked around, I found a piece of glass and decided to cut the window screen out of the motel window to use as a cooking thing over the fire. Well, the screen melted and the hamburgers fell into the fire. We grabbed as much of the uncooked meat as we possibly could. We ate what we could save, even though it had sand all over it. Since most of the meat was uncooked anyway, we just covered it up. Then we decided to make that phone call to the orphanage.

Ronnie and I walked down the beach where we discussed going way out into the water. Maybe we would drown, or be pulled way out into the ocean where a big ship might pick us up. Maybe it would take us to the other side of the world. But I was too afraid to do that, so we just kept on walking. We made our way to a great big hotel with lots of lights. We walked around to the front of the building where all these people were yelling and screaming at one another. Then everything got real still and quiet. We just stood there with lots of other people who were watching this pretty woman with diamonds all over her. She wore a big fur-like coat when she came walking out of the hotel. Then she got into this great big fancy car, and they drove away. Everyone started talking and yelling again for some reason. I saw these men with cameras taking pictures of the car. I told Ronnie that this must be a movie about that big fancy car, and it would probably be on television one day.

I had never seen real diamonds before. That pretty woman had really big diamonds on her ears, neck, and on her arm. I just stood there for a long time, staring at all those diamonds. I thought about how much food and clothes those diamonds could buy for me and the other kids at the orphanage. I turned around to grab Ronnie by the hand, but he was not there. I walked around for a long time looking for him, but I never did find him. In fact, I never ever saw him again, ever. Not even after they took me back to the orphanage.

Ronnie was sad and scared all the time when we lived at the orphanage. So, I think he walked out into the deep ocean all by himself, trying to find that great big ship we talked about. They probably took him to a far away place without any orphanages or mean old matrons, so he could finally be happy.

Killing To Live

Once again, I had made my way across the St. John's River, heading toward Park Street. The city park that I was heading for was located on the opposite side of Jacksonville. It was just about as far from the orphanage where I lived as one could get without leaving town. When I arrived, it was about six o'clock in the evening, and the traffic was starting to die out. I knew the police were still looking for me, because I had not returned to the orphanage after leaving Landon Junior High School four days earlier.

The park was somewhat of a safe haven for us kids when we ran away, mainly because there were many people walking in the park, and many had children with them. The police had learned that it was not easy chasing us orphan kids around the park. Many times, they ended up chasing and catching the wrong kids anyway. The park was dense with trees and large bushes where we could hide. It was a place where we could beg for money and food. If all else failed, there were always the queer men who came searching for young boys almost every evening.

For about four years, I had been taking money from a man named Bill. He was a queer schoolteacher that I met while crossing the Main Street Bridge when I was seven or eight years old. I had just turned twelve, and I think Bill was beginning to think that I was getting a little too old for him, or maybe he thought that I might tell somebody what he was doing to me. However, I had not eaten for two days, and Bill seemed like my only hope for getting food.

I was rather surprised when I reached the park, as there were not many people. Off in the distance, I saw five or six people sitting around in a circle. As I got closer, I saw that it was several homeless people drinking and talking. These are the same people that I generally saw standing around outside the Trailways Bus Station begging for money. I had never seen them in this part of the city before.

"Have a seat," yelled the old woman, as I approached.

Each of them was sitting on an old wooden Coca Cola crate. Over to the side, there were stacks of wooden crates, all broken into pieces. In the center of the group was a small fire with a medium-size black, metal pot sitting atop the fire. I walked over, looked in, and there did not appear to be anything inside the pot, except water.

"Is that there going to be for coffee water?" I asked.

"Don't you know the difference between a coffee pot and a darn cooking pot?" asked the woman.

Every one of them laughed.

Not knowing what to say, I took a seat next to the heavy-set woman. When I sat down, the smell coming from her just about made me gag. I raised my hand to my nose, and I held it there.

"Something wrong with that nose of yours, boy?" said the woman.

"No, ma'am," I replied, as I dropped my hand to my side.

I sat there for as long as I could take the smell, then I stood up, acting as if I had to stretch. I stretched each of my legs, one at a time, and then I began walking to the other side of the group circle, where I took another seat.

"If that damn sun would go down, we'd start us some supper," said the smelly woman.

I looked around to see if I could find any food, but I saw nothing. One of the men had a small duffle bag lying over to one side.

"You going to eat with us tonight?" asked a man wearing a dirty ball cap.

"I'm really hungry. I could sure use something to eat," I responded.

"Good, then it is settled. We need a good, strong young man to get our dinner for us."

I looked at the man, trying to figure out what it was that he meant.

"I can't steal any food for you," I told the group.

"God damn it, kid. Did anybody ask you to steal anything?" said the woman.

"No, ma'am."

"Hey, did you hear the one about the salesman and the farmer?" asked the other woman in the group.

Everyone nodded no.

"Well, this here salesman went to the farmer and told him that he was lost. He asked if he could spend the night.

The old farmer told the salesman that he could, but that he would have to sleep with his youngest daughter. He made it very clear to the salesman that no hanky-panky had better take place. About three o'clock in the morning, the farmer woke up when he heard a loud scream. He ran into his daughter's bedroom, and found that the salesman had jumped out the second-story window, and was now screaming as he ran out across the cornfield.

"What happened?" the farmer asked his daughter.

"That nice man asked me if I wanted to play with his dolly. When I did, it spit on me, and I broke its neck."

The group went into a laugh that I will never forget. The fat woman fell off her crate, and lay laughing on the ground. I just sat there looking at everyone.

"Don't you think that was funny, boy?" asked one of the men.

"I don't get it. Why would a grown man have a girl doll?" I replied.

A complete silence fell over the entire group. Then once again, they burst out in laughter.

"How old are you, boy?"

"Twelve."

"You been locked away in a cave somewhere or something?" asked one of the men.

"No, sir. I been living at the orphanage over by Spring Park School near San Diego."

Once again, the group fell silent. As darkness fell, we each took turns breaking up the wooden crates and stoking the fire to keep it going. Several times, the woman walked down to the public restroom, and returned with water. She carried it in an old coffee can that she had gotten out of the garbage can.

"How come you guys are over here sitting in the park? I always see you standing outside at the bus station," I asked.

"My boy, this is where the food is," someone said.

For the last hour, food was all that I had been thinking about. I kept waiting for someone to open the duffle bag, and take out whatever it was that we were going to cook for supper.

"Well, it's about that time. Come on, boy," said one of the men, as he got up off his crate.

"Where we gonna go?"

"To get our dinner."

I stood up and waited to see what the old man was going to do. He began walking off into the darkness, so I followed him. He stopped when we reached the edge of a large pond. He stood there looking up at the full moon, and then reached into his coat pocket, and he pulled out a slice of white bread.

"Are we going to eat fish for supper?" I asked.

"Hell, no, boy. You be quiet now. I will draw them in with the bread, and then I'll run them toward you. You grab as many as you can, and you twist their necks," he told me.

"Mister, I don't know what you mean," I said, looking rather confused.

"The ducks, the damn ducks," he whispered.

"Ducks?"

"The ducks! We're going to cook the damn ducks."

"You cannot kill these here park ducks. These here is pet ducks."

The man grabbed me by the throat and began to squeeze.

"You help me catch those ducks or I'll push your ass in that damn lake. You got that?"

"I can't kill anything living. Really, I can't."

As the man pushed me backwards, I tripped and fell to the ground. I sat there watching as he began coaxing the ducks close to him using the small pieces of bread he was tossing at them.

"Please, dear God. I do not want to see nothing get dead. Please don't let that man kill those ducks," I prayed.

Well, prayers were not answered that evening. Five minutes later, we were walking back to the small camp. Neither one of us said a word to one another. I stopped about twenty yards from the campsite, and sat down on the ground. The man continued walking. I heard him talking to the others, but I could not tell what he was saying. Occasionally, one of them would turn around and look at me. Therefore, I know he told them what happened. For several hours, I sat there watching as they cleaned, boiled and began eating the helpless creatures. I have to admit they smelled good. I was so hungry that I could hardly stand it any longer. I wanted so much to go and ask them for part of the food, but I knew they would not give me any. Besides, I did not know if I could eat it anyway.

All at once, the six of them got up and began moving around. One of the men took his foot and spread the fire so that it would go out. Then they started walking toward the downtown area. I sat there for about ten minutes before I got up and walked over to where the fire had been burning. There were feathers all over the place. I gathered up a few pieces of the Coca Cola crates, and managed to get the fire started again. I took a stick, and looked through the ashes to see if I could find anything else that they might have cooked to eat. There was nothing.

Several minutes later, I walked over to Post Street, and I knocked on Bill's door. When it opened, he looked at me and smiled.

"Hungry?" he asked.

"Yes, sir," I replied.

"Good!" he said, as he placed his hand on my shoulder.

The Rape

Having run away from the orphanage more times than I could count, I thought I had seen almost every evil thing one human being could do to another. However, on this particular night, that was about to change.

Though I was only twelve years old, I knew quite a bit about sex. What I had not picked up from the boys talking about it in the bathroom at school, I had learned from Mother Winters, the head matron at the orphanage. Little did I know that sex could be a very horrible thing to witness.

All of the boys in the dormitory loaded in several vehicles, and off we drove to get our free haircut at the Florida Barber College located in downtown Jacksonville. Each of us stood with our backs against the wall, waiting to be called when the next available barber chair became empty. I was lucky, because I was third in line. Sometimes, it would take up to three hours for all the boys to get a haircut. Whoever was in the front of the line, after getting his haircut, got to walk outside and sit down on the sidewalk. Every now and then, a few of the barbers would give us a nickel so we could buy a package of cheese crackers from the machine at the store next door.

After purchasing my crackers, I started walking back to the barber college. All at once, I saw a dog running toward me. He jumped up and began licking my face. I kneeled down to pet him, but when I did, he grabbed my crackers and ran away. I began to run after the dog, traveling as fast as I could. By the time I caught up to him, I was several blocks away. I walked around for almost an hour, trying to find my way back. No matter what direction I traveled, I always seemed to end up right back where I started.

After a while, every one of the streets, every one of the stores, and every corner looked the same to me. The more I walked around, the more frightened I became. I knew that I was in very serious trouble when Mother Winters found out I was missing. I stood watching the cars as they passed. I hoped I might see the orphanage station wagon come by, and I could wave them down. There were so many cars passing so fast that, at one point, I became dizzy, and had to sit down on the curb.

"Can I help you?" a man's voice asked.

I began to explain to him that I was lost, and I needed to find my way back. The man walked me the five blocks to the barbershop. I went in, and saw that all the kids had already left. I knew at that moment that I was going to get the beating of my life when I returned to the orphanage. I walked to the small office located in the back, and asked the man to call the orphanage. I stood there listening, while he tried explaining to them what had happened.

"She wants to talk to you," said the man, as he held the receiver toward me.

I reached out, took the phone, and placed it to my ear.

"This is Roger Dean Kiser," I said into the mouthpiece.

"You had better stay right there, you little bastard. You had best not move a muscle. You got that?" ordered Mother Winters.

"Yes, ma'am, Mother Winters," I replied.

Very carefully, I handed the telephone back to the man sitting behind the small desk.

"Why such a sad look," he asked me.

Just as I was about to start crying, I turned and ran out the front door of the barbershop. I did not stop running for what seemed to be hours. Even then, I did not stop to rest. When I was not running at full speed, I was walking as fast as my legs could possibly move. I finally sat down on the wooden steps of a little country store on Old Kings Road. I leaned against the wooden post that supported the small porch roof, and tried to rest for a few moments. After having sat there for about five minutes, the owner of the store came out and sat down beside me.

"What you doing out here, boy?" he asked me.

Not knowing what else to say, I told him the truth. That was not a common thing for me to do.

After hearing my tale of woe, he got up and walked back into the little store. A few seconds later, he came back out and sat a Coca Cola and a package of cheese crackers down on the floor beside me. Then he sat down on the steps, too.

"I don't have no money," I told him.

"It's on the house."

"Why?" I asked.

"Does there always have to be a 'why'?"

"There always is."

Without saying a word, the man stood up and walked back into the store. I sat there staring at the ice-cold Coke and the package of crackers. I looked back when I heard the screen door open again. The man had a broom in his hand, and he held it out to me.

"Here, sweep off the porch, and then eat your snack."

I smiled, stood up, and began sweeping. He watched me as I cleaned between each and every crack in the wooden slats. When I finished, there was not one speck of sand or dust left on the platform. He reached out, took the broom from my hand, and took it back inside. When he returned, he sat down on the steps beside me.

"What you going to do now?" he asked.

"I don't know what to do."

"You've got to make a decision."

"There ain't no decisions that I can make."

"You cannot just sit here for the rest of your life, can you?"

When I heard those words, I did not know what to say. I tried to think, but every thought began to race around in my mind; it was like a never-ending circle of confusion. I sat there staring at the ground.

"I close at six. I'll give you a ride back to the orphan home," he said, as he stood up, turned and walked back into the store.

I just shook my head. At about seven o'clock, the two of us arrived at the front gates of the orphanage. I asked him to drop me off outside the gates, because if I were seen getting out of a stranger's car, I would get an additional whipping. I thanked him, and stood there watching as he drove away. I walked in through the gates and hid myself in the large, thick azalea bushes that lined the white, rock roadway. I sat there until dark trying to make a decision on what I should or should not do.

Finally, I made my decision. I got up, walked back out the gates, and headed toward an old abandoned house that we kids called the old Spanish house—a cement structure that had been vacant for years. It was located in a very nice neighborhood, and was always a safe haven when we had run away from the orphanage. When I arrived, I saw a flicker of light coming from one of the rooms near the back of the building. As cautiously as I could, I entered the house through what used to be the front door. I was hoping I might find several other boys from the orphanage that might have also run away.

"Let's see if we can get her damn bra off." I heard someone say.

I stepped backwards, and made my way out of the house. I cautiously went around the side, and peered through a cement opening. I could smell beer and cigarette smoke almost immediately. There was a very small fire burning in a tin can, and there was not very much light. I could see several men holding a young girl down on the floor in the corner. One minute, she would be telling them to stop and the next minute, the four of them would be laughing, the girl included. They continued to drink one beer after another. The more they drank, the louder they became.

I had been shaking my leg back and forth for about five minutes, because I had to pee very badly. Quietly, I backed up from the opening, and moved into the bushes to relieve myself. When I turned around, a man was standing right in front of me. It scared the hell out of me.

"What you doing out here?" he asked.

"I was taking a leak."

"You like beer?" He asked.

"I have never had any beer before."

"Well, come on in," he said, putting his hand on my shoulder, and pushing me toward the open doorway.

The five of us sat around talking and telling jokes. Everything seemed to be fine. All at once, one of the men got up, staggered, and fell over backwards hitting his head against the wall. He jumped back up and yelled, "Are we going to fuck this bitch or not?"

Every one of them went crazy. The three men grabbed the girl, and began ripping her clothes off. I stood up, backed myself into a corner and just stood there. No matter what, I could not move, and I could not believe this was happening. One minute everything was happy and fun, and now, it was like the lions I saw on television attacking a deer.

"You want some of this pussy boy?" yelled the man, as he climbed off the young woman.

"I ain't never done nothing like that, and I ain't never going to," I told him.

The man walked to the corner where I was standing, and he placed his hands against the wall on each side of my head.

"This is our little secret, right?"

He drew back his fist as though he were going to hit me in the face. I pushed myself tightly into the corner, and slid to the floor.

"Let's get the hell out of here," said one of the men, as he got up off the girl.

The girl had said very little during the attack. Now she lay naked on the floor, sobbing.

"Shut up you little slut whore," said the man who had me backed in the corner.

The man reached down, gathered up her clothing, and handed it to one of the other men.

"Take off your god-damn clothes," the man ordered. Now he was pointing at me.

"I'm not going to take my clothes off!"

Two of the men reached down, grabbed me by my arms, and pulled me to my feet. One of them snatched hold of my shirt, and ripped it off. I struggled as they wrestled me to the ground, and removed my pants and underwear. Then I sat back down in the corner trying to hide my naked body.

Maybe I should fuck this little bastard," said one of the men.

He moved toward me unbuckling his pants.

"Let's just get the hell out of here," said the largest of the three men.

I sat there wondering what I was going to do for clothes. Other than Mother Winters, no female had ever seen me naked before.

"How was I going to get back to the orphanage?" I thought.

The girl and I sat there for almost five minutes before either one of us said a word. I will never forget her first words for as long as I live.

"Is this your very first party?" she asked me.

Breaking Bread

"It is really cold tonight," I thought to myself, as I pulled on the pieces of plastic and cardboard I was using as bed covers for the night. Still, I shivered and I shook for hours and hours, as I lay inside that large, green, rusty garbage dumpster, behind one of the restaurants at the Southgate Plaza Shopping Center in Jacksonville, Florida. I was a big boy now. I had just turned twelve years old several weeks before. I could already smoke a whole pack of cigarettes by myself without choking or coughing, just like a grown up man.

"God, it's cold this time!" I said aloud.

I heard my voice echo off the sides of the dumpster and it sounded very neat to me.

"HELLOOOOOO," I said so that I could hear my own echo again. "God bless America, land that I love," I sang, as loud as I could.

"I sound pretty darn good," I said to myself, as I continued to sing aloud. "Stand beside her and guide her, from the land to the land of the land. GOD! It's really cold," I said again.

I dug a hole further down through the garbage and began to cover myself with food and hundreds of cartons, which had been thrown away during the day. All of a sudden, I heard something scratching inside the dumpster.

"Oh God! I hope that's not another big rat!" I thought to myself.

A large rat had bitten me several weeks earlier over on Riverside Avenue, when I had slept in a dumpster behind the large red brick church.

I took out my package of matches, struck one, and held it forward. Sitting directly in front of me was a large black cat with big, green, shiny eyes. He flipped his tail several times, and just sat there looking at me.

"Meow."

"Are you hungry?" I asked him.

"Meow," he answered.

I reached over and found the container that held four, half-eaten tacos. I'd found them when I first arrived at the dumpster. Carefully, I unwrapped the tacos, and began removing bits of hamburger. I laid the meat out onto a cardboard box next to me. The cat slowly moved over and began to eat the meat. I finished off the lettuce, tomato and cheese, and threw away the taco shells, because they had coffee grounds all over the outside. Then I reached up, closed the dumpster lid, and laid down trying to keep myself warm. The cat moved over next to me and curled up by my neck. I began to pet his back, and he started making a sound like he had a little motor inside him.

"Do you like me?" I asked him.

"Meow," he said.

"I like you, too," I said, as I hugged him real hard.

164

"Who's in there?" hollered someone standing outside of the dumpster.

The lid slowly opened, and I saw a large black man standing there with a gun in his hand.

"What you do in there?" he asked me, shaking the gun around.

"I was just sleeping, sir."

"Where you live?" he asked.

"I live in the orphanage over on Spring Park Road, by San Diego."

"Why ain't you there then? You a runaway?" he asked.

I lowered my head, and remained very silent. He raised his flashlight from the ground, and shone it onto the dumpster.

"Let me sees your face," said the black man.

I covered my eyes, and raised my head.

"Moves your hand boy," he ordered.

I lowered my hand, and looked directly at the light.

"How comes you got a black eye?

I said nothing.

"How long you been coming outs here anyway?"

Still I said nothing.

"You all alone in there?" he questioned.

No, sir. There's a black cat in here with me," I told him. "He is my friend."

"You leave that damn cat in there, and youse get out here real slow like."

I reached over and picked up the only friend I had in the world, held him in my arms, and began to climb out of the large garbage can.

"You don't listen very well, do you, boy?"

I continued climbing out of the dumpster with the large black cat in my arms. When I reached the ground, I hugged the cat, and turned to face the large black man holding the gun.

"You sure stink," he said, waving his hand about his nose. "How long since you had a bath?" he asked.

"I washed yesterday at the gas station," I told him.

He waved his gun to the side and told me to get in his old pickup truck.

"I gotta keep my cat. He's my friend."

"Put him in the truck," he ordered, with a strange smile on his face.

He placed the gun into his pocket and climbed into the old truck. Then he reached over and pushed open the passenger door so the cat and I could enter. I climbed in, and off we drove. About half an hour later, we drove up to an old house located somewhere in Jacksonville, Florida. God only knows where. I had never been to the black part of town, so I had no idea where I was. When we walked into the house, he pointed at the woman and asked her to get him a towel and some soap. He took me by the arm, led me into the bathroom, and told me to get in the tub and take a bath.

"That don't means no gas station washing," he said, pointing at me with his finger.

I sat the cat down on the floor, and the woman came in with a towel and laid it down on the toilet. I took a hot bath and washed very well with real soap. When I was all done, I dressed, picked up my cat and walked back into the front room. The couch and chair were full of holes, and the windows had sheets for curtains. I remember that part very well, 'cause I had never seen anything like that before.

"Have him take his shirt off, Bill," said the woman.

"Take off your shirt," ordered the man.

I sat the cat down on the couch, stood up, and began to remove my dirty shirt.

"Turns around," said the woman, spinning her finger in a twirling motion.

I turned slowly around and stood with my back toward them.

"You right. Someone done got this boy," said the man.

"Who done got you?" asked the large man.

I just stood there with my head down, looking at the black cat that had laid down in one of the large holes in the couch.

"Who do this to you, boy?" asked the woman.

I stood there silently and did not want to answer any questions. I knew very well what they were talking about. Two weeks before, I had been caught eating a box of raisins. We boys had taken it out of the orphanage pantry, while washing dishes at the dining room. Mrs. Winters, the head matron, had beaten me on the breezeway porch with a stalk of bamboo, because I would not tell her who had taken the raisins out of the locked pantry.

The black man walked over to me and placed his large hand on the back of my neck.

"You hungry, boy? he asked.

"No, sir. I had some tacos earlier tonight."

"You gonna eat anyway!" he stated.

We walked into the small kitchen and sat down at the table, which only had two chairs. I do not exactly know what it was that I ate that night, and I do not know if I ever want to know. However, it was hot, it was good, and it did not have coffee grounds stuck all over it. I stayed the night with the man and his wife. I slept on that couch with the big old holes in it, and it felt warm and good.

The next day, the man drove the cat and me back to the dumpster at Southgate Plaza. He handed me four whole dollars and a bag full of corn bread.

"This kind of life is better than the orphanage?" he asked me.

I opened the truck door, picked up my black cat and I said not a word. I closed the door behind me and turned around to face him. I stood there kissing my cat on the back of his neck, as the man shook his head and drove away.

Chinese Drugs

At twelve years old, I was living on the streets of Jacksonville. I was eating out of dumpsters and garbage cans, but only the ones located behind the better restaurants. If you have to be a bum, then you might as well be a high-class bum, or there is no point in living anymore.

I had been given five dollars in the park for letting an old man rub on my leg while he did whatever it is that grown people do when they are rubbing a young boys leg on a dark park bench late at night. I had heard from some of the older bums underneath the train bridge where we slept at night, that the best food to buy was Chinese. It would not spoil as fast, and could be kept for several days without making you sick. Therefore, I walked into a Chinese restaurant to place an order to go. I placed my order and sat down at one of the booths. I was trying to steal as much sugar as I could, and get it into my pocket without being caught. All of a sudden, everything and everyone got very quiet, as four men came walking into the restaurant. One of them was in a police officer's uniform.

It was about three o'clock in the morning. I was really hoping that they would not question me about being out at such a late hour. However, they did not even look at me as they walked by. They just continued down the aisle, turned the corner, and came up the other side of the restaurant. I could not believe how quiet it was. There was not a sound whatsoever. Not even from the kitchen, which had been clanging pots and pans before the men came walking into the restaurant. They made their way down the aisle walking very slowly, looking at each person sitting in the booths. I noticed that a woman stuck something in her mouth. All of a sudden, one of the men yelled out.

"She's got it in her mouth!"

The four men grabbed her and wrestled her to the floor. One man held her head, while the other held her legs and another her arms. The fourth man started beating her in the face as hard as he could. I could not believe that this was happening. There was blood squirting all over her booth, and all over some of the people sitting in the booths next to her. Everyone started yelling, screaming, and running everywhere. I just sat there shaking, too afraid to move. I had not seen anything like this since I left the orphanage the year before. The police officer just kept beating her in the face, until she opened her mouth and spat out a large chunk of food. The officer reached down on the floor and picked it up. He looked at it, and then threw it as hard as he could onto the table.

He looked over at the other man and said, "It's just a damn f'in piece of egg roll!"

"Where are the damn drugs?" yelled another man, dressed in plain clothes.

"We don't have any drugs. We are just visiting here from Canada," said the woman.

The police officer grabbed her by the hair, and raised her off the floor. Then he slammed her back into the booth, and started banging her head against the wall.

"Where are the god-damn drugs?" he hollered.

The man who was sitting with the woman jumped up and pushed the officer away from her. The police officer grabbed his blackjack and raised it into the air. The man sat back down, and shielded his head with his arms. The officer slammed his blackjack as hard as he could down on the edge of the table.

"What the hell is everybody looking at?" he screamed.

People started getting out of their booths, and running out of the restaurant as fast as they could. When I stood up to leave, the police officer looked at me and asked, "Where the hell are you going, boy?"

"To the bathroom. My dad is in there," I told him.

"Then get your little butt in there, and don't come back out," he ordered.

I ran into the bathroom and locked the door behind me, so they could not get me. I sat huddled in the corner for hours and hours. I would not open the door, even when people knocked.

I just could not believe that there were people out in the "real world" that would do this to other people, especially the police. The orphanage did this kind of stuff to us all the time. However, that was 'cause we were orphans and no one cared about us. I knew "Old Topper," the officer who walked around outside the orphanage fences every afternoon, but he was nice. I talked with him all the time through the orphanage fence. He would never beat anyone like that. He was a good police officer.

Well, I knew at that moment that things were not going to change for me in the outside world. I had no idea what I was going to do. I did not have anywhere to go, nor did I have anyone to help me. However, I did know that I would have to get off the streets very soon, because the police would beat me if they caught me. Because I had no place to go, I made the choice to move in with the old man who liked to rub my leg when I visited in the park. He was a schoolteacher and he told me that I could never tell anyone, especially the cops, what he did to me. And I never did.

A Real Thanksgiving

Once again, at the age of twelve, I ran away from the orphanage. It had not even entered my head that tomorrow was Thanksgiving. Thanksgiving Day just happened to be one of the few days when we were given all that we wanted to eat. I was heading out of Jacksonville, and was westward bound, I think. I had been told I was born in the State of California, and that was all I knew for sure. So I figured I had a mother and father out there somewhere.

It was November, so it was getting a little cold as the sun went down. I knew from experience that I could not stay on the main road, as the police would be looking for me. If they found me, I would be arrested and taken to the Duval County Juvenile Hall, or worse, back to the orphanage.

As I walked along, I came across some railroad tracks. I thought I would follow them in hopes they might lead me to my mother somewhere in California. After about an hour or two of walking the tracks, I came across a large bonfire where several men were standing around in a circle trying to stay warm.

"Where you headed, kid?" yelled one of the men.

"Going to California to find my Mom and Dad," I hollered back.

"Going the wrong way, kid," he said, cupping his hands over his mouth like a bullhorn.

I walked over to where the men were standing, and asked if I might get warm by the fire.

"Get that empty can over there, and I'll give you a cup of hot beans," said one of the men sitting on an old stack of tires.

They sure were good beans, too. I think I ate two whole cans. Sure was nice of them to give me some of their food, with them all being poor.

"Might as well stay here for the night," said the man.

He had a sling on his arm. I know my eyes got very big, and I got a little scared when he put his good arm around me.

"It's gonna be okay, kid. I'll look after you," said the man who had given me the beans.

I slept good, considering how cold it was. They had lots of old army-like blankets that smelled very bad. They sure were warm, but they were itchy. The next morning, we had beans once again for breakfast. That was the first time I ever had coffee, and it was really good-tasting. Made you feel very warm inside. After breakfast, we cleaned up our mess, and burnt it all in the fire. We poured water over the fire to make it go out, so that it would not burn anything down.

For most of the day, we walked down the railroad tracks. Occasionally, we would sneak over a fence, and steal some fruit to eat. I did not like stealing, but that fruit tasted awfully good. Right before dark, one of the men went into a small store; he asked if he could do some work for a loaf of white bread and some meat, but the store man told him, "No." Later on, I went back into the store. When the man was not looking, I stole that loaf of bread and two packs of meat, which had bad-tasting pickles in it.

That night, we had fruit, pickle meat sandwiches and beans for Thanksgiving dinner. "Supper," we always called it at the orphanage.

I never knew that poor old people, like hobos, never said grace before they ate, especially after stealing food. However, they did, and they meant it too. I could tell it in their voices when they all said, "Amen."

"Why do you people always say grace when you eat? You are like me. You ain't got nothing to own."

"Ain't you got two arms and two legs, kid?" asked one of the men.

"'Course I got two arms and two legs," I told him.

"Then you got something to be thankful for," said the man, as he raised his pants leg and showed me his wooden leg.

"Did the big war do that?" I asked.

The man did not answer me. He just got up from his seat on the ground and walked away, off into the darkness.

"It's okay, kid. He just takes the war harder than the rest of us. We were all in the war," said his friend.

"You were in the war?" I asked.

He looked down at the ground without answering my question. Then he broke into tears, and covered his face. I sat there not knowing what to say. I just sipped on my warm coffee, and tried to stay warm. The next thing I remember, it was morning.

The four men all told me goodbye. Then they jumped on the slow-moving train, and left me standing all alone beside the railroad tracks.

I walked the ten miles or so back to the orphanage. When I saw the head matron, Mrs. Winters, I told her that I was very sorry, that I had run away, and I was very ashamed for not being thankful for all that Jesus had given me.

"For your warm bed, the food you eat, and the good clothes you wear?" she asked me.

"No!" I told her. "I don't like the food here."

"Then what are you thankful for?" she asked me.

"For my two arms and legs."

"You had best get over to your dormitory before I slap your god-damn teeth out," said Mrs. Winters.

As the days turned into weeks, and the months turned into years, life passed me by. I once again began running away. I suppose because I finally realized that there was less and less in this world to be thankful for.

Donald Watts' Mother

The cars would roll past every now and then. I could see their headlights zoom past, as I lay on the old, dirty mattress in the corner of the small living room. I watched the vehicles through the cracks between the old boards making up the walls of the shack where my friend Donald Watts and his elderly mother lived. Once again, at about eleven or twelve years old, I had run away from the orphanage as I had done many times before. And once again, I had no place in the world to go.

I do not even remember where I met Donald. I suppose it was somewhere on a back street, in the park or in some back alley. I was probably searching for food in a dumpster or garbage can out behind one of the restaurants over on Riverside Avenue.

Just a few minutes ago, I was in the kitchen making a dinner salad for my wife and me, when all of a sudden, and for no reason at all, this thought popped into my head: a picture of Donald Watts' crippled, gray-haired old mother, as she walked out of that run down old shack she called a house. It was a small three-room dump, with white peeling paint that dropped off in large pieces each time the front door slammed—a dirty-looking structure that had light brown pieces of cardboard boxes stuck here and there into the window frames. The glass in the windows had been missing for years, because the property owner would not fix them. It had an old gray roof that leaked constantly, because half the shingles were missing, and had blown away over the years.

I would open my young eyes every single morning, six days a week, when I heard her get up and get ready for work at the Goodwill Store. The woman was so crippled that she was barely able to walk, and had to hobble at a 45-degree angle. She must have been 70 years old or so. I could not believe how anyone her age could possibly be in that much pain, and walk like that day after day, without hurting herself. She could barely get from the living room to the bathroom every night without falling down, much less, make it to the bus stop a block or two away every day. However, she always got up, dressed, and headed out the door at exactly the same time every single morning. This was just to do the job necessary to take care of herself and the two lazy kids living in her home—one of those kids being me. That is the way she had always been from the first time I laid eyes on her. She was just a gray-haired old woman, who was just Donald Watts' mother, so I never gave it a second thought.

I never realized it before today, but that old woman never turned me away or ever pushed me back out into the street, not one time. It had never entered my mind how much that wonderful woman had done for me as a young boy. The little bit of food that they had to eat—and believe me, it was very little—was shared with me equally, and without ever making me feel as though I was imposing or unwanted in their home.

How I miss that old shack today, and that big old plate of burnt mashed potatoes with one piece of white bread. Yes, I said burnt mashed potatoes. There were no pots, so the daily meal of potatoes was fried on the old metal stovetop and then mashed down until they were cooked.

I drove to Jacksonville several years ago. I went to see if the house was still there. When I arrived at the address, all I saw was a large Sherwin-Williams Paint Store. I have searched for years trying to find Donald Watts. I want him to know that I owe his wonderful mother more than a debt of gratitude.

Molding the Orphan

I was twelve years old the first time I was taken to the Duval County Jail in Jacksonville. It was my first time going to jail for running away from the orphanage. Generally, I was sent to the juvenile hall, but I guess after you have run away five or six times, they consider you a career criminal.

This was my first introduction to the "real world," the world outside the chain-link fences of the orphanage.

It appeared that no matter where I went, they caged me like an animal. I cannot say that I was not scared when I entered the jailhouse. Of course, I was always scared when I left the fenced area of the orphanage. I had no idea what was really going on outside of the large wire fences. I was searched and then placed into a large steel cell, with about twenty other men in their late 20s or 30s. After about an hour, several of them started fighting with each another, and guards came rushing into the cellblock to settle the dispute.

When the guards left, several of the men who were playing cards started talking about the "young-stuff," that had just been brought to the cell. Every one of them began staring and laughing at me. The sex talk and the jokes became nasty—really nasty, as a matter of fact.

From the tone of the conversation, I suspected what might be planned once the lights were turned off. I stole a steel spoon from the dinner tray, and slipped it in my pocket. Then I went and lay down on my bunk. Under the blanket, I carefully bent the spoon handle back and forth, until the head of the spoon broke loose from the handle. I figured the handle would make a good knife if it became necessary.

I was scared, and decided when these guys went to sleep, I was going to walk over to the biggest man, and stab him right in the heart with the spoon handle. I would stab him as many times as I could before the guards came in. Finally, everyone went to bed, and I lay there shaking really badly under the wool covers. I just could not stop shaking. I cannot tell you how scared and afraid I was.

I had always considered myself to be a good boy, and I cannot remember anytime during my life—even at the orphanage—when I ever hurt anyone or anything—not even someone's feelings. However, because of fear, I now knew, at age twelve, that I would be able to take the life of another living thing—even a human being. I will never forget that day for as long as I live. I will never forget having to think that thought. That was the first day in my life that I was called to go to war against a civilian population, the population I had heard about that lived outside the fences of the orphanage.

After about an hour, the big, burly, hairy guy finally got up and walked over to one of the toilets. After using the bathroom, he walked back toward me, shaking his large penis as he walked by. He was laughing as he passed my bed. I was one scared little twelve-year-old. Let there be no doubt in your mind. I would have done whatever was necessary to protect my life and myself. At that tender age, I quickly learned what low life sons-of-bitches these so called "loving" human beings really were.

I will never forget that night for as long as I take a breath on this earth. That would also be the last time that I would ever feel that kind of fear. That would be the last time that a tear would enter the eyes of Roger Dean Kiser. That would be the last time I would ever feel anything inside of myself. From that day forward, every decision I would make for the remainder of my life would be made using only the thought processes of my brain. From that day forward, no person would ever control me, tell me what to do, or order me around, ever again.

I would conduct the remainder of my life by calculating every possible situation, computed from every possible angle. I would consider the legal, the moral and the ethical. Even the consequences of the unknown would be taken into consideration as a possibility. There was no room left in this orphan for that ridiculous thing the world called "love." As the years went by, this type of procedure worked rather well. So well in fact, that I began to believe everyone else in the world thought and felt the same as I. It was rather amazing how I could fit in anywhere that I went. I would adjust automatically, without thinking, and meld myself to fit into whatever was going on around me—just as the lizards did at the orphanage. "Animals" like me could change colors at will. I was still one scared little boy inside, but I could play the role, and I could play it well.

I had only completed the sixth grade, and that made my life rather difficult. However, I succeeded by living on the streets mainly because I had such a strong ambition to reach for the top. On the streets, reaching for the "top" is not very high at all. There was no doubt in my mind that my ambition came from feeling less than equal to my fellow man. I suppose that is because of always being told I was a "worthless, retarded bastard."

As I never had a family that I can remember, there was no one in this world for me, except me. Therefore, I could not count on anyone. I had to make it or I would die. I ate out of garbage cans behind the stores, and I slept in old houses where nobody lived. I certainly did not walk out of that jailhouse the next day with any self-esteem, and that is for darn sure.

Anything that happened to me over the next fifteen years did not affect me one way or the other. I thought hard times were normal. That is just the way life is for everyone. I took it on the chin, and I let life roll off my back, just like water off a duck. I never looked back and I always pushed forward. That was all that I knew to do. There was no other way for me.

In spite of all that happened to me, I never became hard, mean or cruel. At least I did not act that way, even though I may have felt that way inside sometimes. I always tried to help my fellow man, and I always shared my food on the street when I saw somebody hungry.

Somewhere deep down inside of me, there was this overriding compassion for humankind—even though I didn't feel anything for him personally or individually. Somehow, in my own mind, I knew how things were supposed to be and that honest-to-goodness people were supposed to love one another. I knew that humans are supposed to be smart, and should care about others, because we all have to live together on this earth.

Still, even to this day, I have never met one human being—male or female—that could get inside my heart and stay there. That day in jail was the beginning of molding this boy into a man.

A Piece of Shit

"He's one of those stupid idiots from over at the Children's Orphanage Home," said one of the boys from my seventh grade class.

I looked him straight in the eye, and he turned his back on me. Then other boys and girls grouped around him and looked away, as if I were not even there. I had hoped that attending a new school located five miles from the orphanage would give me a new start on life. It would be a welcome break from all the jokes and never-ending ridicule that we suffered for years while attending Spring Park Elementary School. It was located next door to the orphanage where I lived.

It took less than a day or two for the word to spread around the classroom that I was from the orphanage. My living in an orphanage home somehow made me different from all the other kids. I could not tell much of a difference myself. However, for some reason, it sure made a big difference to all the other kids in the classroom. For the first week of Junior high school, no one other than my teachers even spoke to me. I sat in my assigned seat just hoping someone—anyone—would smile or speak to me.

I opened up my notebook, and took out a piece of paper. On the paper, I drew a heart. Inside the heart, I wrote the words, "Roger, you are a piece of shit." I folded up the notebook paper, walked to the front of the classroom, and handed the note to the teacher. She opened the paper and began to read the contents. She looked up at me and tightened her jaw muscles.

"You head straight to the dean's office, young man."

She pushed on my shoulder to spin me around facing the door.

"I'm a piece of shit!" I screamed out at the classroom as loud as I could.

Turning, I ran out of the classroom and down the long hallway. I sped to the double doors leading outside the large brick building, and continued to run until I could run no more. I made my way to the St. John's River, and then over to the Main Street Bridge leading back to the orphanage. I stopped when I reached the center of the bridge, looked over the metal railings, and down at the water below.

"That's a long way to fall," I said to myself.

I stood there looking down at the moving water below. I placed my head down on my arms, and just stood there trying to decide what to do. My mind was racing 90 miles per hour. I could not go back to the orphanage, because I had left the school grounds and, as usual, they would beat the pure living crap out of me. There was no way I could return to school and face my classmates, or the Dean of Boys.

"I'm too scared to jump all that way."

Slobber fell from my mouth as I mumbled to myself.

"You have no choice. You're in bad trouble," my mind kept telling me.

"You don't have to jump. Just put one foot up onto the railing," said something inside my head.

Carefully, I raised my foot and placed it on the metal railing, and then I raised my other foot up off the concrete walkway.

"See, that didn't hurt anything," said the voice.

"Yeah, I don't really have to jump if I don't want to?" I said aloud.

"You don't have to jump, if you don't really want to!" said the small voice inside my head.

Each time I took another step, I felt much better inside. The pain and the sadness were disappearing a little bit at a time. Soon, I was half way up the silver steel railing. Now, the passing cars were starting to honk their horns at me. One of the cars came to a complete stop, a man rolled down his window and yelled at me to get down off the railing. I looked over at him and thought to myself. "That man must care about me to honk at me like that."

"Do you like me?" I asked him.

"I like you, son. Come down off that railing."

Slowly, I climbed down off the railing to the concrete walkway below. I have always heard that people who commit suicide really do not want to die. All they want is for the pain to stop. I have never heard a truer statement in all of my life.

The Bank Robbery

I met Donald Watts one evening when he came walking through one of the back alleys of Jacksonville. I had already been living there for almost a week. I was standing next to the garbage can raking my finger around the sides of a can of tuna, trying to get whatever fish might be left inside.

"You ain't eating that, are you?" he asked, as he stopped in front of me.

I was a little embarrassed, and threw the empty tin back into the garbage can.

"If you're hungry, I'll take you over to my house, and I'll get my mom to fix you something to eat."

He turned and began walking away. I followed him, several paces behind. Donald was a much taller boy than I was, but I could tell that we were both about twelve. He might have been thirteen, maybe. I had a hard time keeping up with him, because his legs were so long. After walking for about half an hour, he stopped in front of an old house on the corner of Park and a street I can't remember. I just stood there looking at the old board structure, with its peeling white paint. I had seen old houses before, but this was really old, like a shack. I looked at Donald to see if he might be playing a joke on me, or something. Just about that time, the front door opened, and there stood an old woman, bent over at a 45 degree angle.

"Mom, this is Roger, and he is hungry," Donald told his mother.

"Roger, you come on in this house right this minute, and let's see what we can find you to eat," said his mother.

I followed the two of them into the house, looking in every direction as I walked. Donald and I stopped in the living room, and his mother headed off to the back. The house was very dark inside. There was only light in the front room. It was hanging in the center of the ceiling by an old green cord that had its paper covering falling off. I stood there watching as Donald screwed the bulb into the socket, giving us light.

"Have a seat," he told me.

I looked around, and saw several old couches that had the stuffing falling out. There was a large stuffed chair in the corner, but it had no seat, just old black springs and some cotton stuff.

"I'm going to the bathroom," he said, as he walked toward a dark opening at the end of the living room.

I sat down on the edge of the couch, and watched as he pulled a curtain over the doorway. Finding that strange, I looked around and saw that not one of the openings had a door. I looked to my left when something flashed in my eye. I could hardly believe what I was seeing. I could see the cars passing by, through the boards in the wall.

"How come these here walls ain't got any insides to 'em," I thought to myself.

Donald came out of the bathroom, and asked me if I wanted to sit out on the front porch. I sat down on the unpainted wooden deck, and stared at the traffic.

"Here you go, young man," said his mother as she walked out onto the porch.

She handed me a large plate of fried potatoes, and a slice of bread.

I had not had anything hot to eat for almost a week. I know they must have thought I was a pig. They watched me gobble down the entire plate of food in less than a minute.

"Would you like for me to cook you another plate of food?" she asked.

"No, ma'am. I had plenty. Thank you."

I do not know why or how it happened, but I ended up spending the night with them. When his mother prepared supper, we once again ate fried potatoes with one slice of bread. His mother had a small army cot in the corner of the kitchen. Donald and I slept on several old, stained mattresses on the living room floor. After they fell asleep, I lay there for hours watching the traffic through the cracks in the walls.

The next morning, his mother was up early, getting ready to go to work. Donald had told me that she worked at the Goodwill Store. I did not know how anybody could work on a job, walking all crippled like. It took her a long time to even get from one side of the living room to the other, much less walk to the bus stop and catch the bus to work.

"Donald, you make sure you go to school today, son," she told him, as she headed out the front door.

Several minutes after she left, Donald got up and began getting ready for school. I was already dressed, because I had slept in my clothes. I folded the small mattress, in half and walked out to the front porch to wait for my friend. As he walked out on the porch, he told me I could stay at their house until he got out of school at 3:30 PM. Then he walked down the street, disappearing around the corner.

I sat on the porch for several hours, before I went back into the house to use the bathroom. When I had finished, I began to walk around the house. When I looked around the kitchen, there was hardly any food. There were several bags of potatoes in the corner, and some of them were rotten. There were four or five cans of beans, and a can of carrots sitting on the old wooden shelf. In the refrigerator, there was some cheese and a jar of pickles. I opened the small freezer and found one small package of meat that had ice stuck all over it.

I walked back out onto the porch and sat there wondering. I couldn't figure out why anyone would share their food with me, when they had so little for themselves. I do not know what got into me, but I jumped up and ran down the street until I came to the A&P grocery store. I walked in, walked right up to the man at the meat counter, and said, "I need to get some real good meat, and I need it really bad, too. I'll work hard for it, I really will," I told the man.

The man reached over, picked up a white apron and threw it at me. I just stood there looking at him.

"Get your little butt behind the counter and get to work," he said, smiling at me.

For five hours, I worked cleaning counters, shining glass, and mopping the floor. At two o'clock, I told the man that I had to go. He wiped his hands on his apron, and walked to the front of the store to the cash register.

How much do I owe you?" he asked.

"I don't want no money. I just want food and meat."

"Why do you want food? You're just a kid."

"I got a friend who don't have much food, and his mom is real crippled like. She walks funny, and I need the food for them."

Though I had probably earned less than $5, the butcher gave me almost $20 worth of meat and canned goods. It took me three trips to get all the groceries to Donald's house. I was sitting on the porch when Donald returned from school. I did not say anything to him about the groceries. He and I walked down to the park at Five Points, and watched the ducks swimming in the small pond. When his mother came home, we were sitting on the porch talking to each other. She, out of breath, hobbled up onto the porch, smiled at me and sat down. She opened her purse and took out several dollars.

"Son, you and Roger walk down to the grocery store and get us a small package of hamburger for supper."

"There's a hamburger pack in the refrigerator," I told her.

"Well, I ain't bought hamburger meat in a long while," she said, getting up from her chair and walking into the house.

About a minute later, Donald and I walked inside to get out of the sun. I looked up when I heard Donald's mother coming out of the kitchen. She stood in the doorway, crying.

"What's wrong, mom?" Donald asked his mother.

"Oh, God, did you boys steal all this food?"

"I did not steal any food, really! I was in school all day."

His mother looked directly at me.

"I worked at the A&P all day, and I got paid in groceries," I told her.

Donald's mother sat down on the end of the couch, and cried for more than five minutes. He and I just sat there, our hands folded on our laps, having no idea what we should do. That night, I thought that everyone would be celebrating and happy, but no one said a word as we ate our supper. I watched Donald and his mother scarf down their food in the same manner as I had eaten the potatoes and bread the day before. After supper, Donald and I washed and dried the dishes. Then we joined his mother, who was sitting out on the front porch.

An hour later, Don and I had unrolled our mattresses and were about to go to bed. His mother asked me to come out on the front porch for a minute. She and I talked for almost fifteen minutes. I told her that I had run away from the orphanage several weeks earlier, and that I could no longer take the abuse.

"You are a very good boy. Thank you for the wonderful dinner," she said.

She wrapped her arms around me, and squeezed as tightly as she could. I am not sure what it was that I was feeling at that very moment, but it was a wonderful feeling. For the first time in years, I felt needed, and felt that I had a worth to someone. When she let loose of me,

I looked at her and said, "If you will let me stay here, I will take care of you, if you will take care of me."

Once again, she began to cry. Donald stuck his head out the doorway to see what was happening.

"You can stay here, and you don't have to take care of me," she said.

Donald walked over and hugged his mom. I stayed with them for almost four months. I worked very little during that period, and I contributed very little to our support. Mrs. Watts' income was less than $30 a week. There were just no jobs available for twelve-year-old boys.

Four days before I left Jacksonville, Donald and I were walking down the street. He told me that he wanted to finish school, and get a good paying job—that he wanted to buy his mother a couch and chair that did not have holes in them, and that he wanted to buy her a comfortable bed so she wouldn't hurt so badly at night. He also told me that he wanted to buy her some of those fancy little glass statues that sit on the shelf, like the ones in rich peoples houses.

Late that night, when Donald and his mother were asleep, I got up, went outside, and sat down on the porch. Across the street was a restaurant and small bank. I watched as a car pulled into the bank, opened the night deposit box, and dropped in a small bag. When the car drove away, I walked over and stuck my hand inside the box to see where the bag had gone. The back of the box had a metal plate on the back, so that no one could reach inside. I went back to the house, and lied there all night trying to figure out how to get that money out of the bank.

The next day after Donald and his mother left the house, I spent hours collecting Coca Cola bottles. Late that evening, I cashed them in, took the money and went to the store. I purchased a cardboard box of Tinker Toys, fishing line and ten fish hooks, which I hid in the bushes. The following morning, I walked around the corner to Mr. Lewis' machine shop, where I had him drill holes in each end of the two-inch sticks. I then glued the sticks into a small circle and attached a long fishing line to one of the sticks. Through the other holes, I attached numerous fishing hooks.

Late that night, I sat out on the porch waiting for the car to arrive at the bank. About one o'clock, it drove in and made the deposit. Ten minutes later, I walked to the bank and opened the metal drawer. Holding onto the long fishing line, I placed the Tinker Toy apparatus into the drawer and shut it closed. When I heard the wooden structure hit the bottom, I began pulling the fishing line up and down, until I felt the fish hooks snag something. Then I pulled on the fishing line until I could pull no further. I opened the night deposit drawer and there before my eyes, sat the bag of money. I opened the bag, took out the money, folded it and stuck it in my two front pockets. I took the white bag out behind the machine shop, and threw it in the garbage can, covering it with paper and trash.

After returning to the house, I went into the bathroom, pulled the curtain shut, and counted the money. All together there was $842. The next day, after Donald and his mother had left the house, I walked downtown to Rhodes Furniture. I bought two new beds, a new couch, matching chairs and a dinette set. I paid for the furniture, and then rode with the deliveryman, because I did not know the address of Donald's house. After the new furniture was in the house, and the old stuff hauled away, I walked down to Five Points, where I purchased as many ceramic trinkets as I could carry. I took the little treasures back to the house and sat them in every nook and cranny that I could find.

I took $40 and stuck it in my pocket, just enough money for me to hitchhike to Albany, Georgia later that evening. The remaining money, I put in the freezer for Donald and his mother. I closed the front door of the house, and walked out onto the sidewalk. Slowly I turned around, looked at the old shack, placed my hands over my face, and cried.

Tadpoles

I walked into the mechanical drawing classroom at Landon Junior and Senior High School in Jacksonville, Florida for my last time. I sat at my high desk, and had just finished a note I was going to hand to a girl I had met several days before. As I was about to hand the note to her, this heavy bully-type kid grabbed the note from my hands, started unfolding it, and said he was going to read it before the entire classroom. I got down from my high stool and walked toward him. The entire classroom was silent, including the teacher. I stopped in front of him, looked him straight in the eye and said, "I am going to ask you one time and one time only, to give me back that note"

He laughed and said, "I'm shaking all over."

I cold cocked that big bully right between the eyes, and then landed a right punch directly in the middle of his large, fat, bully face knocking him down to the floor. Blood from his nose went everywhere, including the drawing tables, and all over the students. I reached down, picked the note up off the floor, walked over to the girl, and handed it to her.

"I am very sorry about this," I told her.

I immediately turned around and ran out the classroom door, and down the stairs. When I reached the next landing, a teacher grabbed me by the arm, pulling me to a stop, and said, "Slow down. What's the big hurry?"

"Nothing," I told him.

Just then the mechanical drawing teacher came running down the stairs and saw the teacher holding my arm. The teacher told him to hold on to me until the principal came, and that he was going to call an ambulance as the mayor's son was laid out, all bloody on the classroom floor. I was escorted to the dean's office where I was given five swats with a large wooden paddle, before they even knew the circumstances of the matter. I was then taken to the principal's office where he screamed at me for ten or fifteen minutes.

I sat very quietly with him asking me repeatedly, "Do you realize whom you hit. That is the mayor's son, Bill."

"I don't really care," I told him. "The fat creep is a big bully, and he is no better than anybody else."

"You cannot go around hitting the kids of important people," he yelled.

I stood up and yelled back, "Then you tell me why that fat-ass bully is any better than anyone else. I've been beat on most of my life, and that fat bastard is not going to beat on me or anyone else."

Before he could answer, I started to cry. I ran out of his office, down the large hallway, out of the school, and did not stop for what seemed to be miles and miles. I looked in my pocket and found that I only had 25 cents to my name. I knew that I could never return to the orphanage, and that I had to get out of Jacksonville. Otherwise, I would be beaten to death by the orphanage, or sent to prison by the courts for hitting the mayor's bully brat.

I kept walking for miles and miles with no idea what to do or where I could go. I had just turned 13 years old, and had never really been very far away from the orphanage, even though I had run away many times. I had always tried to stay in that same neighborhood, because I knew my way around. When running away from the orphanage, I had lived and slept in abandoned houses, and underneath the Spring Park Elementary School building.

I went out to the main highway leaving Jacksonville, and stuck my thumb out hoping to catch a ride before the police found me. I walked and I walked and walked, but no one would stop or offer me a ride. Finally, I just gave up and sat down on the side of the road. My legs were sore, and my feet were killing me. It was getting colder and colder as the sun started to set behind the clouds. I sat there for about another hour, and then a big, long, black car stopped in front of me.

"Where are you headed?" yelled this woman.

"I'm going to California," I yelled back at her.

She jumped out of the car, and I ran to get in the front seat between her and the man who was driving.

"My name is Dave, and this is Dee," he said.

"My name is Roger, and I am headed to California," I said to Dave.

"Well we're not going that far, but we will give you a lift to Alabama," he said, winking at Dee.

We talked and drove for several hours, and then Dave told me they were going to stop and get a bite to eat. I told them that I was not hungry, but that I would sit with them in the restaurant. We entered the restaurant and sat at a booth where they ordered chicken and fish dinners. God that smelled so good. My jaws actually hurt from smelling that food. It made the muscles in my mouth move around, and made me drool. I had not eaten since that morning at the orphanage, and then had only eaten one piece of toast, because I was late.

Dave kept looking at me and asking me if I was hungry, and I kept telling him that I was not. I did not have any money, and I was not going to ask anybody for anything. Dave picked up his salad and shoved it toward me saying, "Eat this damn salad. I'm not going to eat it, and it will just go to waste."

I ate the salad, two sandwiches, two desserts, and a large drink they bought me. God was it good! After dinner, Dee and I walked out to the car and stood beside it, waiting on Dave to pay for the meal.

"How old are you?" she asked.

"How old are you?" I asked back.

"I'm 29 and Dave is 30, and how old are you, young man?" she asked again.

I acted as if I did not hear her. I did not want them to know my age or they might call the cops and they would take me to prison, or worse, take me back to the orphanage. A few minutes later, Dave came walking out of the restaurant. He told Dee that it was rather late, and maybe they should get a motel room there by the restaurant. Then they would continue to Alabama in the morning. They asked me what I was going to do. I told them that I would just keep hitchhiking to California.

"You can stay in the room with us, if you would like," Dave said.

It was really getting cold, and I was starting to shiver, so I told him I would stay and ride with them to Alabama in the morning. When we got to the room, Dee went and sat on the end of one of the two beds, and Dave sat down in the chair next to me.

"What do you think of my wife," Dave asked.

"She is very pretty," I replied.

"That is not what I mean."

I did not know exactly what he meant, but I started to get a little scared and uneasy, because the tone of his voice changed.

"I mean how you do like her breasts?" he asked.

I did not know what to say to him. I had looked at her breasts when Dave went to the bathroom at the restaurant, and they looked big in that tight, red sweater. However, I did not say anything, and I did not look at them very long, 'cause that just would not be a right thing to do. Dave got up from his chair, walked over to his wife, raised her sweater and bra over her breasts, and up around her neck. I almost stopped breathing. I was so scared, and could not believe that he had shown another man his wife's breasts. Dave walked over to me and grabbed me by the arm. He pulled me out of the chair toward Dee, who was still sitting on the end of the bed. As I was being dragged toward her, I looked up, and she had a great big smile on her face. All I could see was her big white teeth and those great big, red lips coming at me—lips and teeth that kept getting bigger and bigger the closer I got to her.

When we got to the end of the bed, Dave took one of my hands and placed it on one of Dee's large breasts. I just stood there like a statue, not moving a muscle.

"How does that feel?" he asked.

"It feels like that warm jar of tadpoles I had at the orphanage," I said.

"Who wants a drink?" hollered Dave.

"I do! My mouth is really, really dry," I told him.

I just stood there with my hand on Dee's big breast, afraid to move, or to let go of it.

"I'll get us some Coca Colas," Dave said, as he dropped his change all over the floor.

"Can I go get the Cokes?" I yelled, seeing a chance to remove my hand from the large breast.

"Sure," said Dave, as he handed me all the change.

I walked out of that motel room door, and ran as fast and as far as I could. I hid in the bushes all night long, so that Dave and Dee would not find me, if they drove by going to Alabama.

I am not quite sure what that experience might have done to me later on in life. I did become rather sexually shy after this incident and I had always been very distrusting of adults. At that time in my life, I appeared to be caught, maybe trapped, somewhere between danger and raging hormones. Always having thought that sexual acts were rather a private thing, between a man and a woman, I might have thought that my life was just a little more important than the sex act itself.

This Here Money

I had just turned fourteen, and I was living under the direction of the juvenile court in a small boarding house on Market Street in downtown Jacksonville. On the way home from my job at Murphy's Heating and Sheet Metal Shop, I happened upon a small wood-frame house that was in full flames. Standing out in the street was a woman; her arms wrapped around three small children. Next to her was a man who was down on his knees, his hands covering his face as though he were crying. Within minutes, the fire trucks began to arrive, and people ran in every direction. I just stood watching as the small, wooden house finally collapsed in on itself.

"Do you live here?" a police officer asked me.

"No, sir. I think that woman and that man live here," I told him, as I pointed at the couple.

The police officer walked over and began to question the family. Within thirty minutes, the fire was out, and there was nothing left of the house, except a smoldering pile of embers.

"What's we gonna do?" the woman asked the man, as she too began to cry.

The man just stood there shaking his head back and forth.

"We got nowhere to go," the woman yelled out at her children, as she began hugging them.

"I got this here room at the rooming house. You can stay there for tonight. I'm sure it will be alright," I told them.

The woman said something to the man, and within several minutes, the six of us were walking towards my rooming house. When we arrived, my landlady was standing out on the front porch. As we walked up onto the deck, I could see from the look in the landlady's eyes that something was not right. She told the family to sit down on the wooden chairs, and she asked me to come with her. As we walked down the hallway, I explained to her that the family had nowhere to go, that their house had burnt down, and they would have to sleep outside in the cold.

"There is no way that they can stay here. Those people are Negroes. Can't you see that, young man?"

"But they got nowhere to go."

"That's not my problem, and it's certainly not your problem."

"But what are they going to do?" I inquired.

"Look at me," she said, cocking her head to one side. "It's not your problem, and there is nothing that we can do for them. Now you go out there, and you tell those people that they will have to leave the premises immediately!"

Slowly, I turned around and I started walking back down the hallway. That was the longest walk I ever had to travel. Half way down the hallway, I stopped and I looked back at her.

"Come here for a minute," she told me.

I followed her to the door leading into her room. I stood outside while she went in. Several minutes later, she returned and handed me five dollars.

"Give this to that family, and tell them that is the best we can do."

"Can I see if anyone else will give a little money?" I asked.

"Just this one time, but don't you be doing this anymore, okay?"

"Okay," I said, as I smiled back at her.

As fast as I could travel, I ran from door to door telling the story of the family who had lost everything. Out of 28 rooms, I raised almost $60. When I had finished, I walked back to the landlady's room, and I showed her the money.

"I am really surprised."

She stood there shaking her head back and forth.

"You see there was something that we could do. All we had to do is keep trying real hard." I told her.

"You are something else, Roger Kiser!"

I walked back to the front porch, and I explained that it was against the rules for me to allow anyone to stay in my room.

"There ain't any black people live here, so all this here money came from white people. They all feel real bad that you ain't got no place to go," I told them as I held out the handful of money.

"Everyone who lives here gave money?" asked the man.

"Everyone that was home and in their rooms."

"Can you tell them that they get a free shoe shine, if they come down to the Trailways Bus Station?"

As far as I know, no one ever went to the Trailways Bus Station to collect on that free shoeshine, including myself. However, two years later, I had joined the army and returned to Jacksonville from basic training at Fort Gordon, Georgia. When I walked into the bus station, I saw a man shining shoes. I walked over and sat down in one of the three chairs, and placed my feet up into the stirrups. The man said not a word as he shined my shoes to a glow. After he was done, I got down from the chair, and I held out a dollar bill.

"Don't guess you want that free shine, Mr. Roger?" asked the man.

It took me several seconds before I recognized the gentleman. I slowly stepped down from the high bench-seat, and he and I hugged one another.

"I would be honored to have a free shine." I told him.

I was a Cow Boy

I was not sure exactly where I was heading that day. At fourteen years of age, I had no family, and no place to go. All I knew for sure was that I was an orphan, all alone in this world, that it was cold, and I needed a place to stay. I cannot even remember where I was at that time. If I am not mistaken, I was somewhere in Florida or Georgia.

"Wow!" I said aloud, as I read a small sign stuck in the dirt along the side of the road.

"HELP WANTED. NO EXPERIENCE NECESSARY," read the large, hand-painted sign.

I walked up the long, quarter-mile driveway and knocked at the first house I came to.

"Can I help you?" asked the large man that opened the door.

"I'm here about the no-experience job."

"Have you ever worked on a dairy before?"

"No, sir. I have never worked anywhere before."

"My name is Don. What kind of jobs have you done?" he asked.

"Just criminal kinds of stuff," I told him.

"Criminal stuff! Are you a criminal?" he questioned.

"That's what the reform school told me," I said, looking down at the ground.

"What did you do to be sent to the reformatory?"

"Just running away from the orphanage, and that kind of stuff."

"That was all?"

"I did steal some cigarettes one time. But that was a long time ago when I was a kid."

"Do you know anything about working on a dairy?"

"I know about cows, and stuff like that."

What do you know about cows?"

"You squeeze them on the bottom, and white milk comes out."

"Well, kid, I guess you got the job," said Don.

We walked over to an old white shack. He said it was mine to live in for as long as I worked at the dairy. He gave me a pair of old rubber boots and some gloves.

"You got any belongings?" asked Don.

"What are belongings?"

"Things," he said.

"Things?" I repeated.

"Stuff, clothes and money?" he said waving his hand over his head, and pushing his hair out of his eyes.

"I ain't got any clothes and stuff, and I sure ain't got any money," I advised him.

He pulled out his wallet, and handed me five dollars.

"Walk down to the store and get yourself some food. There are pots and pans in the cupboard. I'll take this from your salary."

He walked out the door.

At 4:00 AM, I will be knocking on your door, so be ready," he yelled back at me.

I walked to the store and purchased a package of hot dogs, a loaf of bread, and a bottle of catsup. I returned to the old shack, got a pan of water, and boiled the hot dogs on the stove. This was the first time that I ever cooked for myself, and I was a good cook, too. Only one of the hot dogs split on the side, so I knew that I was going to be a good cook person. Then I walked around for a while in my very first house before going to bed.

"Up and at 'em," yelled someone, as he began to beat on my front door with his fist.

I jumped out of bed, and my heart was racing fifty miles an hour. I stood up and looked around the room, wondering where I was.

"Get a move on! Get those rubber boots on, and get them cows into the barn," yelled the stranger.

"4:00 AM, cows, milk? What the heck is going on here?" I thought.

As I dressed, it all came back to me. I was a man now. I had a job, a house, and hot dogs to eat. I had to go to work in order to make money. I walked over to the window, and I looked outside. I saw no need for my rubber boots when it was not raining. I locked my front door with my very own key, and walked toward the large barn.

"Open that gate and run those cows into the barn," yelled one of the two men standing in the darkness.

I opened the gate, and then closed it behind me. Waving my arms into the air, I ran around behind the herd of cattle so they would move into the barn. I may not have been the brightest kid on the block, but it took me very little time to understand what those rubber boots were for. I had always thought that stuff on the ground at diaries was just mud that did not smell very good.

We had to milk the cows twice a day, every day, seven days a week, and work from sunup to sundown. After the first few days, I was almost dead from exhaustion. The next morning, I got up and walked out to the barn about two o'clock. The boss had bought several dozen donuts the night before, which I had taken to my house for supper. I stood by the fence eating a donut, when a black and white cow walked right up to me and stood there. I pulled off a piece of donut, and held it out. To my surprise, she walked right up to me, gently took it from my hand, and ate it. After that incident, that cow would always be waiting for me each morning when I came out of the small shack house. I made sure that I kept plenty of donuts at all times, so that she and I could share breakfast together. I had noticed that she had a large, black heart shape on her side, so I named her "Big Hearted Betsy." I would take one small bite of the donut, and then give the rest to her. We did that every day that I worked there.

I was in the barn about two weeks later, when the boss-man yelled at me to come over to his house. When I arrived, he sat down at his kitchen table and said, "Bad news, kid."

"What kinda bad news?"

"Things are bad around here. Got to close the dairy in about a week."

"Cows are giving good milk, Don," I said.

"Lot more to the damn dairy business than just the milk," he replied, shaking his head.

"Do I lose my shack?"

"Afraid so, kid. You finish out the week, and I will pay you then. You were a hard-working criminal kid, so I'll give you a little something extra at the end of the week," he said, as he laughed aloud and turned his back toward me, wiping his face on a handkerchief.

I walked out of the office, and returned to the silo, where I finished shoveling the sour hay stored there. Later that afternoon, I saw a bunch of men driving up in an old pickup truck. They began taking a bunch of tools out of the back of the truck, and carrying them to the far end of the barn.

"What's all them tools gonna do?" I hollered at one of the men.

He said not a word. He took his finger and ran it across his throat like a knife, and then laughed. I did not think anything more about it until I got up the next morning. I did not see the big, silver milk truck that always came to collect the milk. I walked out of my shack, and did not see Big Hearted Betsy at the corral fence. I was surprised when I saw all the cows were already in the barn and that they were in the stalls. I stuck the donut in my front pocket, and headed toward the barn at a very fast pace. I wanted to know who was doing my job, when it was mine to do.

All of a sudden, a strange man grabbed me by the arm.

"Where you headed, kid?"

"Someone's doing my job, and...."

The man grabbed me again, turned me around and pushed me out the barn door.

"You go on back to where you came from. This ain't a place for a kid."

"But I work here for Don, and I got to help milk," I yelled at him.

"Ain't any milkin' around here no more," said the large man. "We're getting ready to slaughter."

"What's a slaughter?"

"Going to turn them into meat steaks."

"You mean kill 'em all?" I yelled.

"That's life, kid. Get used to it," he said, as he turned and walked away.

"You ain't going to shoot them, are you?"

He stopped, turned around, and walked back toward me.

"How old are you, boy?"

"Fourteen, I think."

"Okay. You want to know the truth?" he said, looking directly into my eyes.

"Yes, sir."

"They line them up, and hit each cow in the head with a sledgehammer, and then they cut their throats."

I just stood there in a state of shock.

"But these here are milk cows, not meat cows," I told him, lowering my head and looking down at the ground.

"All cows are meat cows, kid. Got to go and get it done."

He gave me a look of concern, and he walked away. Again, I just stood there in shock. As the man disappeared, I walked into the barn, and found Old Betsy among the herd. I released her steel bar, and I backed her out of the stall, and she followed me out to the corral. I hugged her neck, and then I took the donut out of my pocket and gave it to her. I turned around, walked out of the corral, went back to my shack, and began packing my few belongings. When I walked back out the front door, Betsy was standing where she had always stood, every morning since I had met her.

"Mooooo," she bellowed.

I slowly walked back over to the fence, and reached out to pet her for the last time. Lying on the ground was one small piece of donut, which she had not eaten.

"Mooooo," she bellowed again.

I reached down, picked up the small piece of donut, and I held it out to her, but she refused it. I pushed it toward her mouth again, and again she refused to eat it.

Mooooo," she cried, as she slobbered and shook her head back and forth.

"I can't do it," I told her.

"Mooooo," went her sound again.

I took the small piece of donut and raised it to my lips. I opened my mouth, inserted the one bite of cake, and began to chew. I swallowed the piece of donut, and just stood crying. Old Betsy snorted, turned around, and started walking toward the barn. She never looked back, and finally disappeared into the large doorway. I grabbed my small bag of clothes, my gloves and my rubber boots. I walked over to Don's house, and knocked on the door. When the door opened, I held out my gloves and boots.

"I don't want to work here no more," I told him.

"Come on inside," he motioned with his head.

I walked in and sat down at the kitchen table.

"What do I owe you?"

"Can I have a cow instead of money, and maybe that extra that you were going to give me?" I asked.

"And just what are you going to do with a damn cow?" he questioned.

"I thought I would make her like my horse."

"Look, kid, I am going to save you a lot of grief. Just take this money and forget it," he ordered as he handed me an envelope.

"They're going to kill all the cows anyway."

"Get your butt out to my truck, and I'll carry you out to the highway," he said, pointing at the door.

I got up from the chair, walked out the door, and got into his truck. He drove me down the long driveway to the road and told me to get out. He spun around and headed back down the driveway to the barn. I stood there for about 30 minutes, and then I turned and slowly started walking down the highway. Several miles down the highway, I began to hitchhike. Many cars passed, before a truck finally stopped and offered me a ride. Little did I know that it was one of the men who had slaughtered the cattle.

"Did you get any meat?" asked the man.

"I don't want any meat."

"I got some in the back if you want some."

I looked out the back window of the truck and I saw ten or fifteen packages of meat wrapped in shiny, white, plastic paper. We had driven for about ten miles when the man told me that he had to turn off at the next crossing.

I'll just get off at the corner," I told him.

"Well, I got to pee anyway. Watch my truck and I'll be back in a minute," he said, as he ran off the road, and out into a wooded area.

I walked to the back of the truck and I looked at the packages lying in the back of it. I reached out and felt one of the packages. I jerked my hand back when I felt its warmth. I saw that one of the packages had a note stuck to it that read: "Mark, Lilly phoned and said for you to please pick up some bread, milk and donuts on your way home." I removed the note from the package, and stuck it on one of the other packages. Then I took the package, which had the note attached to it, and I threw it into the bushes along the side of the road.

Several minutes later, the man returned. I thanked him for the ride, and then he drove away. I walked out into the bushes, and I picked up the white shiny package. I got down on my hands and knees, and dug a deep hole in the hard ground. Then I buried Betsy next to a tree, right by the big ditch.

My Friend – The Slut

I was fourteen years old when the court decided to allow me to live on my own. It was either that or I'd be sent back to the boy's reform school at Marianna. The juvenile court had set me up with a job at Murphy's Heating and Sheet Metal Shop. They had also paid for my room for four weeks. It was at a boarding house located on Forsythe Street. That was about two blocks from the juvenile court building.

Every day I would get up at four o'clock, and begin my four-mile walk to the Arlington area where the shop was located. The first week that I walked to work, it rained four of the five days. I was soaked to the bone by the time I arrived. Nevertheless, I worked hard all day, and held my own. Each day after work, I would walk the four miles back to my room, where I would change my clothes. I would then walk down to the Krystal Hamburger, and buy myself five small hamburgers for 50 cents. I would then return to my room, lock the door, eat, and lie on my bed until I fell asleep.

On Friday, I was paid. I asked one of the men that I worked with how I could cash my paper check. He took me into the office, where they cashed it for me. When I got back to the boarding house, I walked up the stairs to my room. As I made it to my door, I noticed that there were three or four sailors standing in the hallway. All of them were drinking beer. They were laughing with one another, and talking very loud. When they saw me, they all walked into the room next to mine, and closed the door.

As I changed my clothes, I could hear them through the wall getting louder and louder. All at once, I heard a girl yell, and then she started laughing. I opened my door, and walked into the hallway. Just at that time, several sailors came out of the room.

"Where you headed, kid?" asked one of the men.

"I'm going to eat some Krystal," I replied.

"Can you pick us up some?" asked one of the sailors.

"Sure."

They handed me four dollars, and told me to bring them back 20 burgers and five French fries. When I returned, I gave them their food, and took mine to my room. Over the next few hours, many more people joined in the party. For hours, they continued to drink. The more they would drink, the rowdier they became.

"Get that damn slut out of here," yelled one of the men.

I heard their door open, and a loud yell. Then I heard someone fall out into the hallway. After their door closed, I slowly opened mine and peeked down the hallway. There was a woman sitting on the floor, her back against the wall. I noticed that her lip was bleeding.

"Are you okay?" I asked her.

"Can you help me to my room?"

I walked out into the hallway, and helped her to her feet. She hobbled as she leaned against my shoulder. Her remaining hand on the wall balanced us as we walked down the hallway.

"I'm in room 20," she told me.

I helped her around the corner to her room. She unlocked her door, and I helped her to her bed. She crawled up onto the bed, and just laid there not moving a muscle. I took the key from her hand, and laid it on the dresser. Then I walked down to the bathroom at the end of the hallway, where I got some toilet paper for her lip. Then I told her "bye," and I locked her door as I left.

As I was returning to my room, I saw three sailors standing out in the hallway, all still drinking beer. A fourth was standing in the open doorway of my room. As I approached, he moved out of my way. Not one of them said a word. As I entered my room, I closed the door behind me, and locked it. When I sat down on my bed, I noticed that my dresser drawer was open. Quickly, I ran over to the dresser and looked inside. My heart raced when I saw that all my money was missing. I sat down on the floor, breathing as hard as I could.

"Oh, God! What am I going to do for food money?" I whispered to myself.

"Those sailor guys stole all my pay money," I said aloud.

I walked back over to the door and opened it. Slowly, I looked out into the hallway, and saw that there was no one there. All at once, I heard a loud commotion around the hallway near room 20. I made my way to the corner where the hallway turned, and peeked around the corner to see what was happening.

"Screw that slut. Let's go," said one of the sailors, as he started down the staircase.

The other two men with him just kept laughing, and banging on her door.

"Open the damn door, you slut," one sailor kept yelling.

I wanted to say something to them about my money, but I was just too scared.

"Come on. Let's get out of here," said one of the sailors.

The three of them headed down the stairs, and out the front door they went. I stood there for the longest time, my face held against the cool wall, worrying about money, and what I was going to do for food. Suddenly, the door of room 20 opened, and the woman came out into the hallway. She walked down to the bathroom at the far end. When she closed the bathroom door, I turned and walked back to my room. I locked my door, lay down on my bed, and started to cry.

"Are you awake?" said a voice at my door.

I wiped my eyes on the bed sheet. Then I walked over to the door and opened it. There stood the woman from room 20.

"Thank you for helping me, sonny. My name is Gloria."

I reached up, and I wiped my eyes as the tears were still running down my cheeks.

"What's wrong?" she asked me.

"Those sailor guys stole all my money."

"Those bastards!" she yelled.

"I don't know what I'm going to do for food."

"Come on," she said as she reached out and grabbed me by the hand.

The two of us walked to her room where she sat me down on the edge of her bed. She picked up her purse, and began to rummage through it.

"Here. Take this," she said as she held out a $10 bill. "If you run short just let me know."

"Thank you, ma'am," I said, as I stood up and took the money from her hand.

"No. Thank you for being kind to me."

She reached over, and pulled me close to her. Then she wrapped her arms around me, and she hugged me as tightly as she could. I remember feeling her warm braless breasts against the side of my face. I stood there in a total state of teenage shock.

"Would you like to spend the night in my room?" she whispered.

"No, ma'am" I told her, shaking my head back and forth real fast like.

"Well, if you change your mind, you just come and knock on my door."

"Thank you for the food money. I will pay you back. I really will."

"I know you will," she said, as she kissed me on the forehead.

I walked out into the hallway, and I turned around to look at her. She smiled at me, and then she closed her door. I stood there for several minutes thinking about what had just happened to me. I wanted so much to knock on her door and tell her I wanted to stay the night. However, I was just too nervous and scared. Even if she did let me back in her room, I would not know what to do or say. I knew about the sex thing, but did not have the slightest idea on how to start the process. Several times, I raised my hand to knock on her door. However, every time I did, my heart would begin to race, and I began to shake so badly that I could hardly stand upright. Slowly, I lowered my hand, turned, and walked back to my own room.

Over the next eight months, Gloria and I became very good friends. She never would take back the $10 that I owed her. In fact, when she had men callers to her room, she would have them pay me to go to the Krystal and pick up food for them. She always made sure that they bought food for me, as well as giving me a great big tip. One Friday, she told me that she was going out of town for the weekend. I never saw her again after that.

Many times over the months, I heard many sailors call my friend "a slut." I am not sure if what Gloria was doing was right or wrong. That was not for me to say. All I knew for sure is that she was a very kind person—a person who cared about me, and she was someone who added much to the life of a very lonely little teenage boy—a boy who had nothing in life to look forward to, except walking to work many days in the rain, and staying all alone in his boarding house room.

Reading Between
The Lines

I am not exactly sure how old I was when the Duval County Juvenile Court finally allowed me to move out on my own. I had already been sentenced to the Florida School for Boys Reform School, mainly because I had refused to ever return to the Children's Home Society Orphanage after my release(s). I believe that I was almost fifteen when they allowed me to rent a room of my own. It was a small room in a two-story, white wooden building located about a block or two from the juvenile shelter.

Somehow, I had managed to get a job at a local sheet metal shop located in the Arlington area of Jacksonville. My room was about eight miles from the shop, and I had no transportation. One of the older men that I worked with told me that he would give me a ride to and from work, if I would give him several dollars a week. The problem was that he missed one or two days of work each week. By the time I walked the eight miles to work, the men had already loaded up the trucks and left the shop.

Every time, Mr. Murphy, the head boss, would tell me to go on back home.

Every day, it was the same routine. I would return to my rooming house, change my clothes, and then walk down to the Krystal Hamburger to get myself something to eat. After eating, I would walk the five miles or so over to Park Street and sit in a small, local park. This was an area of town where my friends and I would gather throughout the years, when I had run away from the orphanage. Some days, no one would show up at all. I would just sit there for hours all by myself. Other days, one or two of my friends would come to the park and we would roam the back streets together.

"Do you know what time the next bus comes?" asked someone walking behind me.

As I turned around, I noticed a young girl about the same age as me standing behind the park bench.

"No, ma'am. I do not know anything about the buses. There's a bunch of them that come by all the time though," I responded.

The girl sat down on the bench beside me, and we began to talk. Over the next hour, she told me about her family, and I told her about my life in the orphanage. She and I talked on and on about the schools that we attended. I was rather a shy boy, and was quite surprised that someone as pretty as she would want to sit and talk to someone like me.

"You sure are awful nice, and you talk real nice, too."

I just sat there smiling from ear to ear. I could not believe that this was happening to me. I just could not believe that someone thought that I was smart, or that I was worth talking to.

All at once I saw my two friends, Donald and Johnny, come walking across Park Street.

"There are my friends coming right there," I told her. "Can you do something extra special for me?"

"What's that?" she questioned.

"Those are my friends, and they both got girlfriends. Can you tell them that you are my girlfriend? I do not mean like a real girlfriend. I know that you cannot say anything like that. But I mean like a girl who's my friend."

She just smiled at me and then she shook her head. By then, both Donald Watts and Johnny Nash had arrived at our location.

"You're sure here early today," said Donald.

"I didn't work again today. I didn't have a ride."

Both Donald and Johnny were now looking at the girl.

"Oh, this is... uh. This is Judy. She's... uh... she's... uh," I stuttered.

"Hi, I'm Judy. I'm Roger's new girlfriend," she blurted out.

She then slid over next to me, and placed her arm on my shoulder. Both Johnny and Donald's eyes got very big. I just looked over at Judy, and I thanked her with my eyes.

I cannot tell you how wonderful that made me feel as a young boy. For that moment in time, everything in the world was wonderful and beautiful. I was so proud that my friends would now know that a girl liked me.

"Well, we're going to the movies. You guys want to go?" asked Johnny.

"I've got to be home by six o'clock," Judy said.

"It's just before four now. You got time," Johnny told her. "If you guys want to go, we'll meet you over there."

Johnny and Donald walked away, and headed toward the theater at Five Points, which was about half a block away from the park.

"I got some money if you want to go to the movie. I'll pay for the movie, and I'll give you this whole dollar for your time," I told her, as I held out a dollar bill.

"Why would you want to pay someone to go to the movies with you?"

"I don't mean anything bad. I really don't," I told her.

She just sat there looking at me somewhat funny like. Well, the four of us went to the movie, and we had a wonderful time. It was the first time in my life that I sat that close to a girl. After the movie, the four of us walked to the bus stop, and waited for the bus to take Judy home. As the bus was pulling up to the stop, Judy looked over at me. Then she looked over at Donald and Johnny who were both staring at me. I just stood there not having the slightest idea of what to do.

"Later, Rog," said Judy.

Then she turned and walked toward me.

"Bye," I said, as I barely raised my hand.

Judy walked over, and she kissed me on the cheek, and then she hugged me very fast.

"Whoa," said Johnny as he slapped me on the back. "How long has this been going on?"

I stood there somewhat in shock, unable to speak. I stood there silently, watching as the bus lights disappeared into the darkness.

"I've been seeing her for a little while now, but it was like a secret. Her family invited me to their house, and we all had a real supper. She is not an orphan like me. She has a real family, and her mom and dad really like me," I lied.

That was the first kiss I remember receiving from a girl. I do not remember a kiss as a little boy. Not even one time; not even by my mother.

I have always wondered why my life took the turn that it did. Was it from all those terrible years in that orphanage, several years in a reform school, and then on to jail? Was it because I went to prison for another three years? Along the way, there were but a few good things that happened to me as a young boy. I think those few things left a "heart-print" somewhere deep down inside of me. Somehow, and for some strange reason, I was able to capture and to hold on to those few precious memories. I was able to use those few kind things as a cornerstone to build a life for myself.

I will forever remember that young girl. She was a very kind, young woman who was able to read between the lines, even though she was looking at a blank piece of paper.

’Til Death Do Us Part

Between the ages of six and fifteen, I had witnessed two murders, possibly three. I had seen at least ten dead bodies lying in the street, all while living on the streets, and running the back alleys of Jacksonville, Florida.

There is no way I could possibly count or remember all the muggings, rapes, and the numerous brutal beatings I witnessed as a young runaway. Homeless people themselves committed several of those murders. A few of them were beaten to death, because they had canned food that they did not want to share. Four were shot trying to steal food or clothing from local merchants. One man had his throat cut because he would not surrender his new shoes. One teenage girl was killed because she made a deal to trade sex for food, and then would not follow through with her part of the bargain. The two men raped her, and then strangled her to death with her own bra.

One young boy was so badly beaten that he had to be taken to the hospital and immediately rushed into surgery. The ten-year-old had been caught stealing beef jerky from a man's shoulder pack. The hobo woke up, and almost beat the boy to death, ripping one of the young boy's eyes out of its socket. I remember standing and watching the entire incident take place. After an ambulance removed the boy, I walked around listening to the adults talk about what had happened. There was not one individual who felt sorry for the boy. Everyone felt that he got exactly what he deserved. There were times that I stole food from various stores, in whatever part of town I happen to be hiding. However, after that night, I never stole anything from anyone living out on the streets.

I remember seeing my first dead body. I am not sure how long she had been lying behind those garbage cans, but the smell was horrible. I nearly threw up. She was blown up like a balloon, and her skin had turned completely blue. Her arm stretched outward and stiff, as if she was reaching for a candy bar or something right before she died. As they loaded her up, I stood there wondering what was missing from her, what would not allow her to move around anymore.

Living out on the streets is very cruel, and a very difficult way of life. The streets will rob you of your childhood even faster than strict parents. The only difference is, strict parents sometimes leave a child feeling hurt, lonely and unloved. On the streets, those types of feelings do not even exist. On the street, you just accept the fact that no one loves, cares or respects you. It is a jungle full of animals, and it is every man or woman for himself; that is understood, without question. The need for love slowly seems to blow away, one grain of sand at a time. Then one day, you wake up, and your need for love is gone completely.

Once kids have lived on the streets, they are never the same, should they ever return home. They pick up feelings of distrust, anger and self-preservation on the street, and that follows them forever. Should they reunite with their family and friends, they become distant, and no longer have a carefree spirit. A learned instinct to protect themselves will not allow their minds to make quick, innocent, childlike judgments, ever again. They will, for the remainder of their lives, sleep with one eye open.

I would suggest to anyone contemplating running away, that he think twice about such an unwise decision. The people you meet on the street may use and abuse you. However, it will be you and you alone, who will destroy your own self. Trying to shed or forget feelings learned out in the street is like trying to forget that two plus two equals four. Once learned, it remains with you forever. The difference being, that "two plus two equals four" is only a thought. They are only numbers stored in the mind to be recalled when needed. The lessons learned from the street are stored in the mind as negative or positive feelings—feelings which, a little bit at a time, turn you into someone that you were not meant to be.

The feelings of distrust and hate that you learn while on the street will remain with you forever and ever. They will travel with you from relationship to relationship. They will follow you from marriage to marriage. You will not be able to shed them, and you will eventually pass those same feelings on to your own children. It is a true case of "'till death do us part."

The Party

After finishing three hours of taping for a television special, I loosened my tie, and headed for my vehicle. Before leaving Florida, I decided to drive by a few of the areas I had hung around in as a young boy.

"Jacksonville sure has changed," I said to myself, as I drove from one area to another.

There was a time when I used to walk from one side of Jacksonville to the other—one mile, ten miles, maybe even twenty miles. Distance seemed to make no difference to me when I was seven or eight years old. Many times, I had just run away from the Children's Home Society Orphanage; I would eat what I could find in the dumpsters, and I would sleep in abandoned red brick buildings along the St. John's River on Riverside Avenue.

I drove over to Post Street, and walked up to the apartment where Bill, the schoolteacher, had molested me after allowing me to spend the night with him. I drove to Spring Park School, which was located next door to the orphanage. I parked and walked over to the orphanage property. I stood there looking through the six-foot high chain-link fence. Other than a few new buildings, nothing had changed. All was quiet and still. There was absolutely no sign of life, and there was no laughter to be heard anywhere.

Next, I drove downtown to see the old rooming house where I had lived as a young teenager. To my surprise, it was gone, and a skyscraper now stood in its place. I walked and walked until my legs began to hurt. I stood for several minutes resting against a department store window, watching the cars as they passed.

"How well I remember those red taillights. Thousands upon thousands of red lights all headed to who-knows-where," I thought to myself.

As it was now past dark, I thought it best that I head back to my home in Brunswick, Georgia.

"Maybe I'll stop in and have one drink before I hit the freeway," I said to myself.

I walked a block or two looking for an open lounge. As I rounded the corner, there stood a man in a suit and tie, holding a door open.

"Are you here for the party? Free food and drink," he blurted out.

I looked in the doorway, and saw about 50 people. All were laughing, holding a drink, and dressed to kill.

"Can you smoke?" I asked the man.

"No smoking allowed in Jacksonville inside any building."

"I'll finish this cigarette, and I might be in," I stated.

"What's life without a party?" said the man, as he closed the door, and walked away to join the others.

I stood there puffing away at my cigarette. All at once, I saw a large flame coming from an alleyway between two large buildings. I walked across Market Street and looked down the alley. I could see four or five people standing around a 55-gallon drum that had a fire burning in it. I stopped, turned around, and looked back at the doorway where the man had invited me to the party.

"Free drinks, free food and intelligent company," I thought to myself.

I stood there for a moment, and then I looked back at the fire. Slowly, I began to walk toward the alleyway.

"Mind if I join you?"

"You a cop?" someone asked.

"No. I'm just plain old me."

No one said a word as I walked up and began warming my hands over the fire. I noticed a few eyes looking at me every now and then.

"You from around here?" asked the large, heavy-set woman.

"No, ma'am."

"Ma'am! Ain't anybody ever called me 'ma'am' for a long time."

The four men began to laugh.

"Sorry," I told her.

"Don't be sorry," she said, rather quickly.

I stood there warming my hands. I remember as a runaway boy standing around many a fire. I did not know these people, but I had known many like them. Many times, these people had fed me when I was hungry. They had given me warmth when I was cold. They had given me friendship when I was lonely.

232

"You got a cigarette I can borrow?" asked the woman.

"No, but I have a cigarette that you can have."

Again, the men laughed. When I held out the package, each person began taking cigarettes, and within five seconds, I had less than five left from an almost full pack. I pulled out my Zippo lighter, and began to light everyone's cigarette. Then I closed it and put it back into my pocket. I placed my own cigarette into my mouth, bent over and lit it from the roaring fire.

"You've done this before. I can tell," said the woman.

"Done this many times, many years ago."

Over the next two hours, we talked, laughed and joked. I was a little uncomfortable at a few of the jokes, as there was a woman present. However, she seemed to enjoy even the coarse ones. Occasionally, I would notice a Cadillac drive up and drop guests at the party across the street. I would watch the women in their full-length gowns enter the building. Then I would look over at the heavy woman wearing her wool overcoat and unmatched tennis shoes.

"You want to pitch in and get something to drink?" asked one of the men.

I had about $200 in my wallet, and wasn't sure if I should pull it out.

"How much are we talking about?" I asked.

"Fifty cents each should do it."

I reached into my pocket and handed the 50 cents to the man. I watched as each gave him his share.

"You want to come?" he asked.

"Sure, why not?"

When we arrived at the liquor store, the man walked right over and picked up a bottle of the cheapest wine. I followed him to the counter, where we waited in line. As I stood there, I noticed a package of clear plastic champagne glasses with push-on pedestals. I reached over and picked up the package. When the cashier got to me, he looked at the wine and the glasses.

"I see you fellows are going to have a real fancy party," he said, as he rolled his eyes back and laughed.

"As a matter of fact we are!" I stated.

I pushed the bottle of wine to the side, and instructed the clerk to give us the largest bottle of Crown Royal that he had in the store. When we returned to the alley, I was surprised that no one said a word about the Crown Royal. I opened the box and removed the bottle from the purple pouch.

"Can I have that there cigarette bag?" asked one of the men.

I threw him the pouch, and he stood there rubbing it against his face. For the next four hours, the six of us stood around the fire talking and telling stories. I watched as each person carefully and slowly sipped his or her drink. Each drank as if he were high society, and had not a care in the world. Then a police car pulled up at the entrance of the alley and threw a spotlight in our direction.

"Let's break it up and get out of there," said the policewoman over the cruisers PA system.

Without saying a word, everyone started walking down the alley in the opposite direction of the police car. I threw my plastic glass into the fire and began walking toward the police. As I passed them, neither officer said a word to me. I just nodded my head and walked across the street. As I stepped onto the sidewalk, I lit a cigarette and stood there looking down the alley. Behind me a door opened, and the man who had invited me to the party came walking out with numerous other guests.

"How did you enjoy the party?" he asked.

"As a matter of fact, it was one of the best parties that I've attended in years."

"Good," he said. "What good is life without a good party and good friends, right," he continued.

"You are so right, my friend," I said, and smiled.

The System Sheds a Tear

I suppose the system will read what I have written, and they will talk among themselves about what a good job they have done. After all, it only took nineteen years of beatings and abuse to turn this orphan into a published author.

I wonder what they will think when they read my writing in books such as *Orphan, A True Story*, *American Orphan* and *The Sad Orphan*. I also have eight stories in *Chicken Soup for the Soul* books. Many stories have been published in the books: *Heartwarmers* and *Heartwarmers of Love*. The two-book series entitled *A Cool Collection* #1 and #2 contains my stories, not to mention hundreds of other books and web sites that have displayed my work. I wonder if they will feel proud, because they—the orphanage—produced an author from their prison. I guess it is only right if they feel proud of themselves and take some of the credit. If not for them, my stories would not exist.

Possibly, I look at things differently than other abused children. Maybe I am just an unappreciative "orphan bastard"—as I was called by many of the matrons—who has not seen the true light of day. After all, I was clothed, fed and housed better than most orphans I know. I do have to admit that the Children's Home Society located in Jacksonville, Florida was one of the most beautiful places in that city. Well, it used to be that way when the slaves—I mean the kids—kept the grounds neat, clean and raked.

I suppose I do owe them a debt of gratitude. After all, they did sustain my life in spite of all the beatings and abuse they bestowed upon me. That is not my major complaint with this or any other orphanage. My complaint arises, because I spent my entire childhood in a confined, fenced-in area located in a great country known as the United States of America. As a child, I was isolated from the outside world, isolated from the real world. And it was that precise world in which I would one day have to live.

The orphanage might as well have been called a prison for small children, because that is exactly what it was. There was never any form of caring, no love, no affection, no kindness, no tenderness, no attention, no gentleness, no generosity and no sympathy. There was absolutely nothing!

The things "free" to most other children, we never had. All we were ever given cost money, such as food, clothing and shelter. What all orphanages overlook is that the "free things" are the spiritual foods that make a child grow and become an upstanding citizen. When orphans grow up, they will give back to society exactly what was received as children and nothing more. That being the case, most likely they will give back abuse, anger and hatred.

However, "the system" does not view it that way. In fact, they still think that in order to get goodness out of a child, they must beat it out of them. They attempt to force good things out of the children. If that does not work, they ship these children off to reform schools, jails and/or prisons. Then the children experience cruel and extreme measures of being turned into confused young criminals.

That is what happened to me and many other orphans living at the Children's Home Society. It really amazes me how orphanages think they can force "two plus two equals four" out of little children, when they never take time to give them the information to begin with. The orphanage, day after day, year after year, keeps on kicking, punching, beating and punishing the children. They never seem to understand that they are not going to get the answer they want. The children cannot give them the answer they want, because they do not know it. The only thing that the children can give them in the end is a very unhappy and lonely result.

Figuring out the problem is not difficult at all. How can a schoolteacher do a good job teaching, if she has 60 to 80 children in her classroom? She cannot. So how does the orphanage expect a houseparent to love 60 to 80 children? That cannot be done either. So what does the orphanage do? They do absolutely nothing. The children will just have to learn to live with the problem, thinking the entire time they are better off in a bad situation, rather than living on the streets. The orphanage feels that there is no problem to be solved, as long as no one is complaining that a problem exists.

Even the orphan children do not realize that a major problem exists. They will not realize that until they become adults. These orphan children think this type of treatment is a normal way of life. They do not realize children living outside the orphanage have a much better life. What we really have here is a very beautiful "puppy mill." Believe me, everything looks pretty darned good from the outside.

It is true that most of today's orphans are fed, clothed and housed as well as children who do have parents. However, the real story goes so much deeper. This orphan thing has become really big business. It is composed of many people, each playing a role, and each acting like a big shot. They plan their little parties, drink wine and eat cheese, while pretending to do wonderful things for the community. Many people are on the payroll, as are their friends. Each one of them paid big bucks to meet and party at the Marriott Hotel. The entire time, they pat each other on the back, hoping no one will see what is really happening.

Please do not think that I do not appreciate what I was given. That is not what I am talking about here. I am talking about all those wonderful people who run home after their meetings, grab their own children, and give them a great big hug and a great big kiss, before tucking them into bed. Yet the very kids that they strive to help, the very children that they work for every day have never had a hug or even a kiss, before being sent to bed. And more often than not, generally they were sent to bed in a harsh manner.

I remember Bill Stroud breaking his arm when he fell off the top of the boys' building. He was not treated like a little boy with a broken arm. He was treated like a thing that needed to be fixed. Therefore, they beat his little ass, and then they fixed him. The last I heard of Billy Stroud, he was serving time in the Florida State Prison at Raiford. That is one tough joint. Bill Stroud was the best looking boy in the orphanage. This boy today, could be right up there in the top of television soaps. Instead, he is a convict with a broken arm. I am not saying that Billy Stroud should not have gone to prison. What I am saying is this: Bill Stroud's life took that direction, because of a lack of compassion and love from the Children's Home Society in Jacksonville.

Gee, who would ever think this would happen to Billy? He was clothed, fed, and housed so well. I wonder if a great big hug and a great big kiss would have made a great big difference in his life.

I guess what is not understandable to me is this: when these children start to branch out into society, they have not been prepared to be lovable, kind, considerate, understanding or gentle. All they know is how to get along with the group, the bunch, the herd and the gang. This "gang" is their family. The teachings, feelings and emotions that are present in the normal family household are non-existent in the orphanage. These emotions do not happen automatically; they are taught throughout the years.

You cannot take a wolf raised in the wild, drop it into the middle of downtown Jacksonville, and expect it to eat at a fancy restaurant using good manners. It just is not going to happen.

I can tell those of you that have no idea what living in an orphanage is like that it is like your first day of kindergarten. Your parents drop you off, but they never come back—ever. You will sleep, eat and live in that school building. You will not leave for the next fifteen to eighteen years. You will never enter a mall or a store of any kind. You can stand by a window and cry your little eyes out, but no one cares. No one gives a damn. You can feel sad and lonely all you want. No one cares. However, I will tell you this: when it is time to eat, you had better have your little ass in that chow line or you are going to get pure living crap knocked out of you.

Of course, your teacher is going to do the best she can to care for you. She will treat you well. However, do not expect any of this love thing. There are 80 other kids in your class. She does not have time to coddle you. Even if the teacher does love children, how can she love all 80 of them? She cannot. Therefore, she gets use to it. Just sit your little ass down and shut up.

Besides, how is she going to control all of these children? She can only control the mass of children by doing one thing. She must make every child, no matter what age, do exactly the same thing at exactly the same time, every day, year after year. Can you even imagine having to live like that? Can you imagine having to go to the bathroom when someone else decides you have to go? You are forbidden to decide when you have to use the bathroom. You are forbidden to think on your own. Thinking will be decided for you.

The teacher knows that if any child were allowed to think on his or her own, it would throw the entire class into a state of chaos. God forbid that a child should begin to develop into an individual person. Such a thing cannot and will not be tolerated.

Can you imagine having 80 little individuals running around doing their own thing, each being his own little person? Each one trying to think in a different direction, and all are doing it at the same time? Well, it happened to us orphans. This is when they sent these evil kids off to the reform schools, jails and prisons.

As I said, this orphan stuff is powerful business, and I stress the word "power." The normal growing up process is viewed by the orphanage as a disruption to the unit as a whole, and cannot be allowed under any circumstances. A boy sneaking into the clothing room to get a long pair of pants for his first day of high school was not a criminal. The boy who climbed up the big oak tree in the center of the orphanage grounds was not a criminal. The boy who took a bike from the girls' dormitory to experience his first bike ride was not a criminal. The boy who dug a hole to make an army fort was not a criminal.

Oh, yes, the boy who sent Elaine Smith that little note telling her how much he liked her? He was not a criminal. That one I will never forget, probably because that was the first time my heart was ever broken and totally crushed. I was made to feel like a sex fiend or a pervert at the age of ten. I was simply a little boy growing up. It was not a man wanting to do the wild thing. Evidently, the orphanage could not tell the difference.

I will never forget the time they locked me in the heater room. I was accused—guilty actually—of looking at Vel Addison's crotch when she came out in those tight, white short pants. That was not a criminal act either. It was just a young boy starting to develop normal human feelings for another human being. There was no one to help us kids direct or redirect those thoughts and feelings.

There was no one to explain these were normal feelings, but that they must be contained.

I remember the first and only dog we ever had at the orphanage. I have no idea where she came from. We named her Honey, a big, old, ugly bird dog that was brown and white. We loved that dog, and that dog loved all the kids. I will never forget being told that a car outside the orphanage gate had hit Honey. I would not walk out that gate for fear of seeing Honey lying dead in the road. After school, Mrs. Winters, the head matron, called me to the office. She made me go out and, with my bare hands, pick up pieces of Honey from off the road. I will never forget that sight for as long as I live. It was worse than horrible. Her insides were all over the place. I was covered with her blood from head to toe. I will never forget the look on Honey's face, as she lay dead. I knew that dog would never love me again. I cried the entire time.

Again, those of you who are not orphans will not get the true message. Having to clean up my own dead dog was not the point. The fact that there was no one who gave a damn how we children felt is the real issue. There was never anyone to hold us, or tell us that everything was going to be all right. There was never anyone who gave a damn if our little hearts were ripped apart. The orphanage only saw a dead dog in the road and a bunch of whining, little bastards.

Conclusion

What was it about the people that I met on the streets that caused me, later on in life, to hold on to my positive experiences, rather than to the negative ones? Once I finally ran away from the orphanage, was I such a lonely, hard-hearted little boy that no one could break my spirit. Maybe no one had ever taken the time to give me a spirit. Why did the kindness shown to me by a few mean so much? How did the kindness of some overpower the beatings, the molestations and the abuses that I suffered from others?

Considering my abusive childhood, many psychologists have told me that I should have become an alcoholic and/ or a drug addict. The doctors are somewhat puzzled. The answer to that question is very simple. I choose not to do drugs or alcohol, because I was afraid that doing such things would allow someone to take advantage of me. I have always had to stay alert and vigilant in order to protect myself. I trusted no one to look after me or take care of me, should I have too much to drink. If I were to become drunk, would my friends take my money, and leave me where I lay? Would they take my car, and continue with the party?

What caused me to think in such a manner? Did I develop these traits, because of my abuses while living in the orphanage? Was it because of my experiences while living on the streets and back alleys of Jacksonville, Florida? Maybe it all boils down to nothing more than a mental deficiency.

I suppose the real question is: why did I not turn out to be some type of a serial killer?

Considering my past, I guess I fit the profile. Even had I thought in that manner, whom do I decide to kill? What about Mrs. Jones who owned the trophy shop? How about Mr. Jenkins, the local gas station owner? What about doing away with the garbage man who spills my trash all over the road each week?

Why would anyone want to hurt someone who had absolutely nothing to do with what happen to him? Even if you found the people who were responsible for your abuses, and you sought vengeance, what would that change?

Therefore, if this is the case, and if this is how I truly think, considering I have a very logical mind, there was absolutely nothing left for me to do, except build a life based upon the good feelings that I have for those who were kind and helped me. Oh, how much that kindness meant to a little boy who had nothing—absolutely nothing at all.

Thank you for letting me share your fire-barrel, and warm myself when I was cold. Thank you for sharing your can of beans and your hot coffee when I was hungry. Thank you for teaching me how to survive, and how to protect myself. Thank you for being my friend, before they killed you for food. Thank you for teaching me how to labor, so that I would no longer have to steal to feed and clothe myself. Thank you for teaching me how to think, and for convincing me that I was not retarded, as the orphanage said. Thank you for teaching me that one must give as well as take. Thank you for taking the time to teach me that I had a worth and a value to the world. Thank you so much, my friends, for giving me those positive feelings, so that I could one day build an honest life for my family and me. Thank you for changing my life.

Yes, there are many lessons I learned from the streets. Those lessons, together with never wanting anyone to feel the pain or the sorrow that I felt as a little boy, is what formed me into the person that I have become today.

Was it worth all that I had to suffer? I would have to say that it was not the best of experiences. However, it was most likely one of the smartest decisions that I have ever made in my life, mainly because it changed the future of my offspring. Neither my children, nor my grandchildren will ever have to know what it is like to eat from a garbage can, or warm their bodies standing around a 55-gallon barrel.

Overall, it was a very high price for an innocent little boy to have to pay—all caused by the irresponsible actions of his selfish parents.

However, in the end it is "you" who will have to make the final decision. It will be "you" who will have to pay the price of being unhappy for the remainder of your life. It will be "you" who ran so fast, trying to find yourself that you did not take the time to stop, just for a moment, and look behind yourself and notice that no one was chasing you, except you.

Roger Dean Kiser

About the Author

By the age of four, Roger Dean Kiser had been abandoned, first by his parents and then his grandparents and placed in a Florida orphanage. Unable to adapt to the difficult, often cruel and abusive environment of the orphanage, and stigmatized by his repeated attempts to run away, he was transferred to a Florida reform school at age twelve. Roger's poignant recollections of his painful childhood experiences will take you into the heart of a child abandoned by his family and abused by the system responsible for his care.

Now an adult, Roger Dean Kiser writes about his childhood along with his current day tales. A real-life Tom Sawyer, Roger's stories find a common ground in each of us. Roger Dean Kiser is a simple man with only a sixth grade education yet he possesses a wonderful ability, storytelling.